How to
Measure Achievement

D0372808

Lynn Lyons Morris
Carol Taylor Fitz-Gibbon

Center for the Study of Evaluation
University of California, Los Angeles

Ⓢ SAGE PUBLICATIONS Beverly Hills/London

The *Program Evaluation Kit* was developed at the Center for the Study of Evaluation, University of California, Los Angeles. Copyright of this edition is claimed until December 31, 1988. Thereafter all portions of this work covered by this copyright will be in the public domain.

The *Program Evaluation Kit* was developed under a contract with the National Institute of Education, Department of Health, Education and Welfare. However, the opinions expressed herein do not necessarily reflect the position or policy of that agency, and no official endorsement should be inferred.

The *Program Evaluation Kit* is published and distributed by Sage Publications, Inc., Beverly Hills, California under an exclusive agreement with The Regents of the University of California.

For information address:

Sage Publications, Inc.
275 South Beverly Drive
Beverly Hills, California 90212

Sage Publications Ltd
28 Banner Street
London EC1Y 8QE

Printed in the United States of America

International Standard Book Number 0-8039-1067-3
Library of Congress Catalog Card No. 78-58656

ELEVENTH PRINTING, 1983

Table of Contents

Acknowledgements

How To Measure Achievement is part of the *Program Evaluation Kit.* The kit contains eight books, each covering a topic commonly confronted by evaluators of educational programs. The kit was developed over a three year period as a project of the Center for the Study of Evaluation (CSE), University of California, Los Angeles, funded by the National Institute of Education. Many people besides the kit's authors contributed to its eventual publication either conceptually or through technical support.

The idea of writing such a kit we owe to Marvin C. Alkin, Director of CSE from 1968 to 1975. Eva L. Baker, current Center Director, provided the continuing solid support and lively interest necessary for its completion. Adrianne Bank, first as co-director of the kit project in its early stages and finally in her role as the Center's Associate Director, gave us the moral support necessary to traverse the arduous stages of kit production.

Several staff members aided in the kit's extensive field test—151 sites throughout the United States and Canada. We thank Margeret Dotseth, Marlene Henerson, Richards Smith Williams, and Esther Goldstein for their painstaking work in gathering and organizing field test data.

The kit books were extensively reviewed by experts in the areas of evaluation research, methodology, and measurement. Comments on an early draft of this book were made by Jason Millman, Cornell University; Alexander Law, Chief, Office of Program Evaluation and Research, California State Department of Education; and Rodney Skager, Jennie Yeh, and Rand Wilcox, all of CSE. Valuable advice and information on the content of this book were graciously given by Clinton Walker, Director of the CSE Criterion-Referenced Test Evaluation Project. The test selection procedure in Chapter 3 reflects much of his thought. Michael Bastone not only edited an extensive portion of the final manuscript, but contributed critical comments and content throughout its preparation.

The authors wish to thank members of the Center's technical support staff who worked hard to keep manageable the production of such a large work. Donna Anderson Cuvelier carried the major responsibility for typing, organizing, and supervising manuscript preparation. Ruth Paysen ably shouldered part of the burden of typing the extensive manuscript. Proofreading and indexing were handled by Robert Murar and Mark Young.

Thanks are also due to Lou Orsan of Visual Sense, Inc., who provided advice about graphic design during preparation of the field test draft of the kit and who designed the books finally published.

We wish finally to thank Cheryl Tyler of the UCLA Office of Contracts and Grants who ably ushered the kit through final legal channels toward publication.

Lynn Lyons Morris

Carol Taylor Fitz-Gibbon

Los Angeles, California
August 1978

Chapter 1

Measuring Achievement for Program Evaluation: Preliminary Considerations

The objective of this book is to help you determine how well the program you are evaluating has met achievement *objectives*—usually those mentioned in the program's official description but possibly others added to your measurement plan for one reason or another.[1] The book intends to support you toward this aim in two ways: (1) it provides suggestions, procedures, and rules of thumb for performing evaluation tasks related to measuring achievement for program evaluation; and (2) it introduces some of the *theory* underlying the procedures for developing and selecting achievement tests and interpreting their results.

The book's contents are based on the experience of evaluators at the Center for the Study of Evaluation, University of California, Los Angeles, on advice from experts in the field of educational measurement, and on the comments of people in school, district, and state settings who used the field test edition. Wherever possible, procedures are presented in a step-by-step format. This should give you maximum practical help with minimum theoretical clutter. Keep in mind, however, that many of the recommended procedures described in this book are methods for selecting, administering, and interpreting achievement measures *under the most advantageous circumstances.* Since few evaluation situations will exactly match those envisioned here, however, *you should not expect to be able to duplicate exactly the suggestions in the book.* It is hoped that you will examine the principles and examples provided, and adapt them to the press of your own time constraints, the context of your evaluation, and your data requirements.

---

1. Any one of a number of situations could prompt you to measure achievement of skills other than those mentioned in official program objectives. For instance, you might want to look at side effects—achievement of skills related to but not included in the program. You might also decide to check whether participation in the program has brought about a *slowdown* in achievement in a curricular area *not* emphasized by the program.

An underlying objective of this book is to help you, through your own work, to improve practice in the new and growing field of evaluation. While most evaluations fall short of providing absolutely clear information on the worth of programs or program components, the task of any one evaluator is to provide the best information possible. This means gathering the most highly credible information allowable within the constraints of your situation and presenting the information to each of your evaluation audiences[2] in a form that makes it useful to them. Your task with respect to the program's achievement goals is *to provide each audience with descriptions of the amount of achievement the program seems to have produced, supported by evidence that the achievement measure you have used is sensitive to the program's objectives and likely to be giving you accurate information.*

Each of the book's six chapters deals with one area of practical advice. The list of orienting questions in Chapter 1 should help you decide what to measure and how much time and effort to invest in measuring achievement. The chapter and the whole book deal with achievement *tests.* While some evaluators might choose to assess a program's cognitive effects through less orthodox means—say, through rating of student projects— most measurement issues in educational evaluation center around formally developed tests. Besides, the principles discussed in the book are general enough to be applied in almost any situation where information about achievement is collected and reported.

The topic of Chapters 2 and 3 is selecting and obtaining published tests. Chapter 2 describes the types of achievement test data that might already be available—from curriculum embedded instruments and state- or district-mandated measures. It discusses ways in which they can be useful for your evaluation. It also lists sources of published tests that you can buy or borrow.

Since many evaluations will require that you use an already published achievement test, you will need a basis for choosing one or for determining the appropriateness of the test that you are required to use. In the interest of providing a partially quantitative method for estimating test appropriateness, Chapter 3 presents a *Table for Program-Test Comparison*

----

2. *Audience* is an important concept in evaluation. The audience is the evaluator's boss; she is its information gatherer. Unless she is writing a report that will not be read, every evaluator has at least one audience. Many evaluations have several. *An audience is a person or group who needs the information from the evaluation for a distinct purpose.* Administrators who want to keep track of program installation because they need to monitor the political climate constitute one potential audience. Curriculum developers who want data about how much achievement a particular program component is producing comprise another. Every audience needs different information; and, importantly, *each maintains different criteria for what it will accept as believable, credible information.*

(TPTC). Following a step-by-step procedure to complete the table, you will be able to calculate *indices* of relative test appropriateness to the program you are evaluating. These indices show the match between the test and the program's most important objectives, the *proportion of these objectives* that the test covers, and the *proportion of the test's items* that are relevant to the program.

In some cases, where time and money allow, you might want to construct your own test. Chapter 4 is a guide to resources to help you custom-design a test to fit your evaluation. It references *How To* guides on the topic of test construction and item writing. It contains, as well, an annotated list of test item and objectives banks in various subject-matter areas, and a list of testing services who will design and score tests for you.

Chapters 5 and 6 deal with technical quality and *use* of tests. Chapter 5 discusses reliability and validity issues in achievement testing. Chapter 6 contains a short discussion of test interpretation and score reporting.

Evaluator Roles

The *Program Evaluation Kit,* of which this book is one component, is intended for use primarily by people conducting *program* evaluations. As a program evaluator, the amount of effort you invest in selecting, constructing, administering, and scoring achievement instruments—as well as the amount of information you need to collect concerning each instrument's measurement accuracy—will be largely determined by the *role* you play with respect to the program being evaluated. Your job will take on one of two shapes depending on the task you have been assigned. In some cases, you may find that you are to assume some of the duties of each:

1. You may have responsibility for producing a *summary statement* about the effectiveness of the program. In this case you probably will deliver a report to the program's funding agency, a government office, or another representative of the program's constituency. In this report you will probably be expected to describe the program, to produce a statement of its goals, to estimate the extent to which these goals have been achieved, to note unanticipated outcomes which the program seems to have produced, and possibly to compare it with alternative programs. If this description fits your job, you are a *summative evaluator.*

2. Your evaluation task may assign you the role of *helper* or *advisor* to program planners and developers. You may then be called upon to examine the program as it develops, identify areas where it needs improvement, spot potential problems, describe for the benefit of the staff the nature of program activities, and perhaps periodically test participants' progress in achieving cognitive or attitudinal goals. In this

situation you have many jobs, all demanding that you work with the project staff to help them produce the best possible program. You may or may not be required to write a report. If this loosely defined job role seems closer to yours, then you are a *formative* evaluator.

The information about the design, administration, and interpretation of achievement measures contained in this book is intended for use by both formative and summative evaluators. Your perspective on the measurement of achievement will vary, however, depending on which of the two roles is yours.

The Perspective of the Summative Evaluator

The summative evaluator's primary interest is to find and use instruments which measure whether the program obtained *its overall goals*. For this reason, the summative evaluator must pay close attention to the program's announced and apparent achievement objectives. He is interested in designing or purchasing measures which are most sensitive to determining the accomplishment of these objectives. The summative evaluator's interest in describing the program's overall impact on achievement should extend, as well, to a concern for measuring cognitive gains which seem to be occurring but which program designers have not mentioned among their objectives.

The summative evaluator may have additional reasons for measuring achievement. If he is using an evaluation *design* to determine the extent to which good outcomes can be attributed solely to the program, then he may wish to use an achievement test for assigning students, classrooms, or schools to program and comparison groups.[3] This common use of achievement information, called *blocking* or *stratified sampling,* assures that the groups produced will be, at the outset, as alike in prior achievement as possible.

The summative evaluator may receive a request to include in the final report not only a statement of the program's achievement of its own objectives, but also an indication of how participants in the program now compare in their achievement with people in other schools or districts. In these cases, the evaluator needs to select, administer, and report the results of achievement tests that provide such normative data.

Because the summative evaluator produces a report which could affect important decisions about the program's future, he needs to ensure *high*

3. Discussion of evaluation designs can be found in most texts on the topic of educational research. See, in particular, Fitz-Gibbon, C. T., & Morris, L. L. How to design a program evaluation. In L. L. Morris (Ed.), *Program evaluation kit.* Beverly Hills: Sage Publications, 1978, and also Campbell, D. T., & Stanley, J. C. *Experimental and quasi-experimental designs for research.* Chicago: Rand McNally, 1966.

credibility in the instruments he produces or purchases. That is, he must use instruments that his evaluation audiences regard as appropriate and accurate.

The Perspective of the Formative Evaluator

By contrast, the formative evaluator's reasons for measuring achievement are less official. Usually, the formative evaluator's major responsibility concerning achievement measures is to make *progress checks* throughout the course of the program and to ensure that students are learning what is expected and keeping to the anticipated pace. The primary audience for this information is the program's staff and planners. Because of their intimacy with the program, staff members will usually not insist on demonstrations of the technical excellence of the instrument, though of course they will want to be able to trust what it tells them.

Another task of the formative evaluator may be to conduct short experiments to try out program components or to settle controversies among planners about which versions of program implementation will work best. In these situations the formative evaluator selects or constructs tests which measure the *specific achievement objectives* of the components under scrutiny.

Because of less rigid data collection requirements, the formative evaluator can be more flexible than the summative evaluator in choosing achievement instruments. The *end-of-unit tests* which often accompany curriculum materials, for instance, are usually suspect as measures of program achievement for the purpose of summative evaluation because such tests may too narrowly focus on the particular program materials used. Consumers of summative information generally want to know whether the program has taught skills that can be successfully used in *other,* non-program situations. For formative evaluation, however, unit tests are ideal data collection methods; they tell the staff whether students are at least learning what the program materials contain. In general, *the formative evaluator can assess achievement using whatever method she and her immediate audience perceive as providing credible evidence.* Of course, if the formative evaluator finds herself producing measurement instruments to settle controversies among the staff about alternative ways to implement the program, the need for technically defensible measures will again become critical.

If a *summative* evaluation is in the program's future, then, an additional aim of the formative evaluator might be to find or produce achievement instruments which have wide credibility, while still presenting a fair picture of the program's effects. To this end, the formative evaluator can collect unit tests, teacher constructed tests, and instruments from related curricula, trying these out during the course of program development to look for items sensitive to achievement of the particular program's objectives.

The formative evaluator may want to collect data that will *stimulate discussion* among staff members and planners. Monitoring student progress in achieving program objectives can prod the staff to set more reasonable expectations about what the program can accomplish in the time during which the students are exposed to it. By measuring achievement of skills which are *not* mentioned among the program's stated objectives, the formative evaluator can point out where the program is producing unanticipated learning or where it is deflecting attention from another area in which achievement may be slipping. The formative evaluator's strongest contribution to the program could turn out to be the discovery of important skills necessary to program success—skills which the program did not take into account—or the identification of abilities which the program indeed produced by which had not been identified as program objectives.

Whether you are reading this book with a formative or summative evaluation in mind—or for professional growth—*How To Measure Achievement* should make you familiar with major issues and tasks surrounding the design and use of achievement instruments for program evaluation. Should you wish to explore achievement measurement in greater depth, you will find suggestions for further reading at the end of most chapters.

Types of Tests

Hardly anyone has taken more than a few steps into the field of evaluation without hearing about the distinction between criterion and norm-referenced tests. In fact, achievement tests available for conducting an evaluation come in *at least* two varieties. In order to appreciate why different sorts of tests have been created, some historical background is necessary.

How Norm and Criterion-Referenced Tests Came About

The first tests used on a large scale and developed systematically were *norm*-referenced. They were used for sorting people into, say, IQ groups and Infantry and Officer Candidate School nominees. For the purpose of this discussion the primary distinctive feature of these tests was their method of scoring—scores were relative. Since the purpose of the test was to compare people, simply knowing that Recruit Burns got 32 items right was not helpful. So the tests were *normed*; that is, they were administered to large groups of people and the distribution of their scores was graphed. Knowing how a norm group would score enabled test developers to convert "32 right" to a standard, comparative score. If, for instance, 75% of the norm group had scored lower than 32, then Burns scored at the 75th percentile. For choosing and sorting people, this is more useful information.

The *method of development* of norm-referenced tests (NRTs) was determined by their use. They needed to discriminate among people. Typically, the process of developing an NRT went—and still goes—something like this:

1. A broad and general area of human performance is chosen as the topic of the test. Usually this topic area or "construct" is reflected in the test's title: *Academic Attainment, Scholastic Aptitude, Modern Language Proficiency, Manual Dexterity.*

2. To ensure that the test covers the construct's major manifestations or adequately represents curricula in widespread use, the test developers survey the subject content and arrive at a range of cognitive or affective behaviors that can be formed into test items. A *content/process matrix* is frequently used to organize this survey of possible kinds of items and to focus attention on how many items—and therefore how much weight—should be assigned to each sub-area of the construct. An example of a content/process matrix used to plan a unit test in Spanish is presented in Table 1. It shows the various topics covered by the test and the relative emphasis given to each. While a *local* test developer wants his test to reflect the objectives emphasized by a particular teacher or program, the commercial NRT developer tries to arrive at a balance of coverage by building content/process matrices that reflect various textbooks and curricula in common use.

3. For each sort of item called for in the plan, a large number of candidate items is written.

4. Items are tried out on an appropriate group of examinees, and item statistics are computed. Each item included on the final version of the test is required to do its part to produce scores that rank people. Statistical methods of item analysis are generally used to eliminate items that decrease the efficiency of the test in producing this ranking. The difficulty index,[4] calculated per item, allows the test developer to weed out items that too many people pass or fail, and retain those passed by close to half of the examinees. Good *item discrimination* is another property that norm-referenced test developers want their in-

---

4. Item difficulty is *zero* if all the examinees got the item wrong, and it is *one* if all the examinees got the item right. Otherwise, it ranges from .01 to .99, reflecting the proportion of the tryout group that succeeded on the item.

TABLE 1
Content/Process Matrix for a Test in Spanish

| | PROCESSES | | | | | |
| | Listening | | Reading | | | |
CONTENTS	& Translation to spoken English	& Response in spoken Spanish	& Translation to written Spanish	& Response in written Spanish	& Translation to written English	TOTAL
Expressions of quantity	1 #B-1*	2 #B-4, B-5	2 #A-1, A-2		1 #A-22	6
Time of day	1 #B-2	2 #B-6, B-7	2 #A-3, A-4		1 #A-23	6
Dates	1 #B-3	2 #B-8, B-9	2 #A-5, A-6		1 #A-24	6
Usage: por/para			2 #A-7, A-8			2
Usage: ser/estar		2 #B-10, B-11	3 #A-9, A-10, A-11	2 #A-16, A-17		7
Number and person: gustar		1 #B-12	1 #A-12	1 #A-18	1 #A-25	4
Idioms with hacer, tener, poner			3 #A-13, A-14, A-15	3 #A-19, A-20, A-21	3 #A-26, A-27, A-28	9
TOTAL	3	9	15	6	7	40

*Cells show number of items and item numbers for each area of content which the test measures.

struments to have. An item discrimination index[5] shows to what extent high achievers on the test did better on a given item than low achievers. In order to locate flaws in multiple-choice items, test developers may check to see which of the incorrect alternatives were avoided by most or all of the examinees.

With the rise of individualized instruction in the 1960's, curriculum designers discovered that they needed tests for monitoring the progress of the students. In order to allow a student to progress through a program of instruction, educators wanted to know at various junctures precisely *what the student knew,* and whether he knew *enough* to go on. This would mean meeting a standard or criterion level of performance.

It became clear to a number of people, notably Glaser,[6] that the techniques for generating NRTs were unsuited to this purpose. For one thing, they were not designed to examine *the amount of subject matter known*; they were intended to decide how well a student's general academic performance compared with that of other students. They were *referenced* primarily to the *norm* group, and only secondarily to the *subject area.*

Because of this, NRTs had two more specific problems as well:
a. The presence of items that were good discriminators, while considered a great asset of NRTs, could penalize a student who had learned well enough to progress further in the curriculum but not so well as to overcome the *trickiness* in some NRT items. Some measurement experts felt, in fact, that item selection procedures based on discrimination indices for NRTs had removed just the sort of straightforward items one would want a unit test to contain.
b. The rather loosely constructed content/process matrix method for designing NRTs made it difficult to say exactly what a person who did

---

5. There are really several indexes of item discrimination. All can be similarly interpreted, however. The values assumed by an item discrimination index can range from -1, through zero, and on up to $+1$, just like a correlation coefficient. In fact, the meaning of the index is like that of correlation, since a negative discrimination index for an item tells you that results for that item correlate negatively with performance on the test as a whole. Specifically, those who did well on the entire test tended to get that item *wrong*, while those who did poorly on the test tended to get the item *right*. You can imagine that an item with a negative discrimination index would be an embarrassment to a test writer, since such an item is apparently measuring something different from the test as a whole. A discrimination index of zero is not such good news either, since it means that those who failed the test did just as well on the item as those with the highest scores. In most cases, an item must have a positive discrimination index in order for it to be useful on a test that must differentiate among examinees.

6. Glaser, R. Instructional technology and the measurement of learning outcomes. *American Psychologist,* 1963, *18,* 510-522.

well actually knew. He knew a little of this and a little of that; but did passing a proficiency test in Spanish, for instance, mean that he could correctly conjugate the language's most commonly used irregular verbs? NRT scores were inadequate for determining conclusively whether students had learned *specific* skills.

In the late 1960's, test designers began to produce tests to help educators detect what students had learned in given subject areas. Since these tests would be used to determine whether students had *mastered* instructional objectives, the tests were called *criterion-referenced*. Students passed them by attaining or surpassing the score pre-set as a *criterion* of sufficient knowledge or skill.

Of course, classroom teachers have informally made both criterion- and norm-referenced interpretations of tests for a long time. A teacher, for example, may have given a 20-item spelling test. If the teacher decided that the top 10% of the class should get A's, then he was using a norm-referenced interpretation. If he decided that any student who misspelled fewer than three words should receive an A, his interpretation was based on a performance criterion. What has been noteworthy about the criterion-referenced testing (CRT) movement during the past 15 years is its development of techniques for designing and using CRTs more effectively *on a large scale* and for purposes, such as state-wide competency testing, that transcend the individual classroom.

The desire to set criteria of proficiency in particular skill areas led to new approaches to test *construction*. If test scores were to show specifically what students had learned, publishers would need methods for planning tests that were much more detailed than the content/process matrix. This led measurement experts to the concept of *domain-referenced* testing. A domain-referenced test is one that is assembled by sampling in a prescribed way from a well-defined set of items that measure an instructional objective. One advantage of using such a test is that it provides a clear means of generalizing about what an examinee knows. If Alisa got three out of four items right on a domain-referenced test, we are justified in saying that she could get about three out of every four items right on all items from the same behavioral *domain,* that is, from the class of all items that *could* have been on the test as described in the *domain specification.*

A domain specification prescribes the exact nature of the items that are candidates for the test. This prescription includes:

- Instructions to the examinee and other conditions surrounding test administration
- The extent to which item components may vary, down to details of permissible vocabulary, formats, and the characteristics of distractors for multiple-choice items
- Objective scoring procedures

During test tryouts, item selection depends on pass or fail patterns only to the extent that items which students *do not understand* are discarded or revised so that they become comprehensible.

If your evaluation will require that you construct your own achievement test, some of the references in Chapter 4 on the topic of domain-referencing may interest you. As yet, unfortunately, no commercially published tests have been developed through domain-referencing techniques; but some have been developed for well funded curriculum evaluations and research.

Because of the various uses to which tests have been put, and because by now at least two technically well-developed methods exist for producing tests, vocabulary about types of tests has become confused. The following definitions are intended to clarify the terms used in this book to designate different approaches to testing in education.

A *norm-referenced* achievement test is an instrument whose content has been drawn from a general body of subject matter or a variety of curricula in a given subject; its items have been selected for their ability to discriminate among examinees; and its scores are interpreted relative to the performance of one or more norm groups.

A *criterion-referenced* test, as used here, is a mastery test—an objectives-based measure that has cut-off or criterion scores used to make decisions about the examinee. Each group of items based on a single objective produces a score that yields a pass/fail judgment. In most cases, the cut-off score for mastery is determined by an educated guess, but research studies and statistical methods can make it possible to say, with a measured degree of confidence, that students have mastered the skill in question when they have successfully responded to a certain proportion of items on a test of a given length. A CRT can be used to assess individual student progress or prerequisite learning as well as to evaluate the strengths and weaknesses of programs, teachers, or educational products. It *is* possible for norms to be established for criterion-referenced tests; and while such norms give added meaning to the test scores, they are secondary to the mastery-of-objectives interpretation of the scores.

An *objectives-based* test is one whose items measure achievement of intended learnings in a particular area whose sub-areas have been phrased as objectives. The test may or may not employ cut-off scores, and it may even be a norm-referenced test. Items for these tests are developed according to the specifications of the objectives they address. The only feature making these tests objectives-based is that each item is keyed to a statement of an educational objective that encompasses what the item measures.

A *domain-referenced* test is one designed according to the precise item prescriptions dictated by a set of domain specifications. The domain specifications describe the stimulus to be given to examinees, the response expected, and the scoring criteria to be used. Three benefits accrue from the detail with which domains are described and the way in which items are sampled from domains:

1. The difficulty of the test is not left to be determined by the item writer. For complex cognitive skills involved in reading comprehension and problem solving, for example, ordinary behavioral objectives do not give sufficient guidance to test developers, so that whether an examinee answers an item correctly may depend on who wrote the item. Domain specifications circumscribe the elements that make items more or less difficult, and the sampling plan ensures that the same balance of more and less difficult items will appear on parallel forms of the test.

2. Domain specifications make clear what instruction will be necessary in order for students to respond correctly to items from the domain.

3. The score on the test serves as an estimate of the proportion of items from the domain that the student can get right. The domain-referenced score, therefore, gives evidence about the *degree of development* of a particular skill. Although mastery levels can be set for domain-referenced tests—making them criterion-referenced—they need not be. When a score tells you that a student can successfully solve about 75% of a particular type of problem, that is valuable information in itself.

NRTs and CRTs For Program Evaluation

The growing consensus among evaluators is that, in general, criterion-referenced tests serve evaluation purposes better than do norm-referenced tests. Norm-referenced tests are useful for gaining indications of the *overall* performance of students, but they fail to reveal strong and weak points in instruction—information which is usually of interest to the formative evaluator and may concern the summative as well. While norms are extremely useful in some evaluation situations—most often summative—where you might want to compare program students' performance with external comparison groups, norm-referenced tests have been criticized as being insensitive to some of the gains that students make through program participation.

In general, a *norm-referenced* test will serve your evaluation purpose:

• If you are seeking to select program participants and need a test that differentiates among people

• If you wish to match or block students, classrooms, or schools prior to assigning them to a program, and you want to base this matching on measures of general ability or comparative achievement

• If you plan to use test results to compare performance of program participants with that of a nationwide or local norm group.

When you want a test that will be maximally sensitive to the changes in student achievement brought about by the program, then you are advised to consider using a criterion-referenced test keyed to the program's objectives. There are myriad reasons for this advice. One is that regardless of the relevance of some of its items to the program, a norm-referenced test usually has to be administered in its entirety in order for you to validly interpret scores in the manner described in the test manual. On the other hand, criterion-referenced tests are designed to be broken into parts according to the objectives that the items measure, so you can freely pick and choose items with no loss in interpretability of results.

Another reason for using CRTs in program evaluation is that some NRT items which discriminate well among students tend to be "oddballs." They contain some twist that students who know the material might still fail to see. This criticism is an attack on the validity of using the norm-referenced test for determining what students understand or can do. Presumably, then, NRTs might be measuring something else in addition to the objectives described in the test manual. Some writers have speculated that this "something else" is *test wiseness* or a certain kind of cleverness that picks up cues which are independent of the content or skills on which the test should focus. Also, where students have equal proficiency in a subject, it will be the quicker and brighter students who complete more items accurately. Some critics of NRTs have gone so far as to claim that the reliability and validity of norm-referenced achievement tests derive in large part from the contribution that general ability makes to test results.

Not all experts agree with the criticisms leveled against norm-referenced tests. Proponents of norm-referenced tests argue that while items are ultimately selected for their ability to discriminate among students, the discrimination provided by the test enables it to distinguish students who have learned the subject well from those whose knowledge is so weak that they must go slowly.

While the controversy over the various advantages of criterion- and norm-referenced tests rages in the background, many evaluators are choosing to use criterion-referenced tests where possible. In situations where it is important to know in detail *what* students can do and *what* they cannot do, criterion-referenced tests simply yield clearer information.

Some Critical Questions

The major reason why a program evaluator—either formative or summative—measures achievement is because the evaluation audience is concerned about whether the program is meeting written or unwritten achievement *objectives.* Before you make any decisions about *how* to collect your information, therefore, you will need to examine these

achievement objectives in the light of the following questions, each of
which raises issues which must be considered before you proceed.

Question 1. What Use Will Be Made of the Achievement Information?

Your answer to this question will determine the amount of time and effort
you should spend on measuring achievement. If you are a formative
evaluator, ask yourself whether program staff or planners are indeed
committed to making program changes based on your evaluation. Will
program alterations result from the findings you report about student
progress or from short experiments you are able to conduct? Will people
be willing to discuss and take note of the achievement information you
provide? In other words, will the information you supply make a
difference?

The summative evaluator should consider *who* will read the evaluation
report and what this audience will do with the information. Could the
summative information reach a newspaper? Might it be used as an ax to
eliminate the program or as a promotional wedge to increase its acceptance? Or has past experience shown that summative evaluation for this
particular evaluation audience is merely *pro forma*?

Of course, prior to reporting your information, you can never be
completely sure about how it will be used. On the other hand, you cannot
help but use a projection of its influence to determine whether you should
invest more or less effort in measuring achievement.

For one thing, anticipation about the potential influence of the information will affect decisions about whether to seek new and better achievement measures or use available tests and easily obtained achievement
information. If you discover that your measure of the achievement of
program objectives could result in drastic changes or even termination of
the program, then you must make a commitment to find or construct a
measure of program achievement that is not only valid and technically
acceptable, but that also measures the achievement objectives *fairly*. A
measure that is *fair to the program* is one which is relevant to the major
information or skills taught by the program *as it was actually implemented.* However, in summative evaluations where the program's planners
and staff have promised a program that would accomplish a set of
pre-determined objectives—say, to raise reading level by a certain amount
within two years—*fairness to the program's constituency* requires that
these objectives be a primary focus of the evaluation.

Question 2. What Objectives Will Guide Selection
or Construction of the Achievement Measure?

In order to be useful as a reference for selecting an achievement test or as
underlying organizers for constructing one, objectives (or in their absence,
curricular outlines) need to meet the following four criteria:

A. Objectives should be clearly stated

How clearly depends, of course, on whether you will use them for test selection or test construction. Objectives used to guide test selection should be stated precisely enough so that it will be clear which tests more nearly measure the skills addressed by your particular program. If the objectives will be used to underpin *construction* of the test, then they must meet more stringent criteria—they should be so specific that several test item writers working from the objectives would produce nearly identical tests.[7]

There are several places where you might locate objectives adequate to guide a search for the appropriate achievement measure. One approach is to examine the *written instructional materials* being used. Publishers are, with increasing frequency, prefacing these with lists of objectives and detailed curriculum outlines. Still another source of objectives is the growing body of *objectives collections* available for purchase. Some sources of these are listed in Table 2.

In some cases, you may wish to *write the objectives yourself*. If time is short, if the program's subject matter is highly specialized, or if your assessment will be fairly informal, this may be the best strategy. A few interviews with the program planners and a look at the program in action should give you a good idea of the objectives toward which the program is aimed.

B. In order to produce a test that is relevant to the program, objectives should be verified against the program's implementation

Programs that aim toward many objectives often put into practice activities to accomplish only some of them. In most cases, before choosing a test, you should be careful to distinguish between the objectives actively pursued and other "official" objectives which for one reason or another have been shelved. The long lists of ambitious objectives that accompany official statements of programs are often written because program planners have prepared a proposal for a funding agency. Such proposals need to promise great things in order to be placed in contention for funding. Sometimes, too, highly ambitious objectives are symptomatic of the aspirations of naive planners. Once a program has been implemented, harsh

---

7. Several books are available that direct the statement of objectives for the purpose of guiding instruction or constructing tests. See particularly: Morris, L. L., & Fitz-Gibbon, C. T. How to deal with goals and objectives. In L. L. Morris (Ed.), *Program evaluation kit.* Beverly Hills: Sage Publications, 1978. Gronlund, N. E. *Stating behavioral objectives for classroom instruction.* New York: Macmillan Publishing Co., 1970. Mager, R. F. *Preparing instructional objectives* (2nd ed.). Belmont, CA: Fearon Publishers, 1962. For a discussion of domain specification, that is, provision of objectives so behavioral that they precisely describe test items, see Popham, W. J. *Criterion-referenced measurement.* Englewood Cliffs, NJ: Prentice-Hall, 1977.

TABLE 2

Sources of Measurable Objectives
in a Variety of Subject Areas

Clark County Curriculum Guides	available from: Clark County School District 2832 East Flamingo Road Las Vegas, Nevada 89121
Course Goals Developed by **the Tri-County Project**	available from: Commercial-Educational Distributing Services P.O. Box 8723 Portland, Oregon 97208
Elective Quarter Plan **Curriculum Materials, Grades 1-12**	available from: Director of Curriculum Jefferson County Board of Education 3023 Melbourne Avenue Louisville, Kentucky 40220
Evaluation for Individualized **Instruction (EII) Pool of** **Behavioral Objectives and Test Items** **for K-12 in Language Arts, Math,** **Social Science, and Science**	available from: Institute for Educational Research 1400 West Maple Avenue Downers Grove, Illinois 60515
Individual Pupil Monitoring System **(IPMS) Behavioral Objectives Booklets** **for Grades 1-6 in Reading and** **Grades 1-8 in Mathematics**	available from: The Test Dept. Houghton-Mifflin Company 777 California Avenue Palo Alto, California 94304
Learning Objectives and Behavioral **Objectives (Primary, Secondary,** **Junior College)**	available from: Cambridge Book Company 488 Madison Avenue New York, New York 10022

TABLE 2 (continued)

Measurable Objectives Collection in Many Subjects for Grades K-12	available from: Instructional Objectives Exchange Box 24095 Los Angeles, California 90024
Objectives and Items for K-12 in Language Arts, Math, Social Science, Science, and Vocational Education	available from: The Co-op 413 Hills House North University of Massachusetts Amherst, Massachusetts 01002
Specimen Set of *Mastery; an Evaluation Tool* for Reading and Math, Grades K-9	available from: Science Research Associates, Inc. 259 East Erie Street Chicago, Illinois 60611

Sources of Broadly-Stated Goals and Goal Categories

Brochures of Objectives in Art, Career and Occupational Development, Literature, Mathematics, Music Reading, Science, Social Studies, and Writing	available from: National Assessment of Educational Progess 700 Lincoln Tower 1860 Lincoln Street Denver, Colorado 80203
Taxonomy of Educational Objectives, Handbooks I & II	available from: David McKay Co., Inc. 750 Third Avenue New York, New York 10017
Workshop Packet for Educational Goals and Objectives	available from: Phi Delta Kappa, Inc. Eighth Street & Union Avenue Box 789 Bloomington, Indiana 47401

reality forces the staff to reduce the number or difficulty of the objectives on which teaching efforts will focus. By looking at the program in operation and discussing the objectives you plan to measure with the program staff and possibly even with students, you should finally find a test that assesses the achievement gains of the program that actually occurred.

Even when your purposes as *summative* evaluator is to produce a test that matches the program's "official" objectives, you should not ignore program implementation. The program should be given a chance to look as good as it can in achieving those objectives it does address.

C. Objectives should reflect the level of skill attainment which the program hopes to produce

How an objective is phrased is critical for test selection or construction. The skill represented by a general program objective can be mastered by a student at different depths. These different amounts of mastery will result in the display of increasingly complex test behavior. If the level of performance is specified in the objective, then the test items will call for correspondingly appropriate responses. Too often objectives describing a program define skills at a lower or higher level than they are actually taught in the program.

For example, a science program may be attempting to teach basic concepts at an elementary level:

> *. . . when asked, the student will express that photosynthesis is the method by which plants nourish themselves.*

Then again, if the curriculum aims toward more complex skills, the science program might want to produce deeper understanding:

> *. . . The student will write an essay describing the conditions under which photosynthesis occurs.*

The program might even seek to develop quite advanced abilities:

> *. . . the student will describe, via an essay and appropriate equations, the chemical processes occurring during photosynthesis.*

Most programs seek to develop various skills and attitudes at different levels of attainment, and the test that is selected or developed should reflect these levels. The Taxonomy of Educational Objectives developed by Bloom et al., and outlined in annotated form in Table 3, identifies several levels of knowledge and understanding. Someone familiar with the program should review the objectives with such a taxonomy in mind before the objectives are used as a framework for prescribing an achievement test.

TABLE 3
An Annotated Cognitive Domain Taxonomy*

This classification describes, from simplest to most complex, six degrees to which information that is taught can be learned.

1. **Knowledge.** *Recalling information pretty much as it was learned.*
   In its simplest manifestation, this includes knowledge of the terminology and specific facts—dates, people, etc.—associated with an area of subject matter. At a more complex level it means knowing the major sub-areas, methods of inquiry, classifications and ways of thinking characteristic of the subject area, as well as its central theories and principles.

2. **Comprehension.** *Reporting information in a way other than how it was learned in order to show that it has been understood.*
   Most basically this means reporting something learned through an alternative medium. More complex evidence of comprehension involves interpreting information in "one's own words" or in some other original way, or extrapolating from it to new but related ideas and implications.

3. **Application.** *Use of learned information to solve a problem.*
   This means carrying over knowledge of facts or methods learned in one specific context to completely new ones.

4. **Analysis.** *Taking learned information apart.*
   Analysis means figuring out a subject matter's most elemental ideas and their interrelationships.

5. **Synthesis.** *Creating something new—and good, based on some criterion.*
   This creation can be something that communicates to an audience, that plans a successful goal-directed endeavor, or that subsumes a collection of ideas within a new theory.

6. **Evaluation.** *Judging the value of something for a particular purpose.*
   This means making a statement of something's worth based either on one's own well-developed criteria or on the well-understood criteria of another.

*Adapted from *TAXONOMY OF EDUCATIONAL OBJECTIVES: The Classification of Educational Goals: HANDBOOK 1: Cognitive Domain,* by Benjamin S. Bloom, et al. Copyright © 1956 by Longman Inc. Previously published by David McKay Company, Inc. By permission of Longman Inc.

D. Objectives which underlie the test should be of high priority

You may find yourself facing long lists of objectives. Many programs, particularly those involving design of an extensive curriculum, perhaps for several grade levels, embody myriad objectives. It is not unusual, in fact, for programs based on installing a commercial curriculum to encompass hundreds of objectives or, where objectives are absent, separate curriculum topics. You of course cannot test all of these, and you need to ensure that the test you do develop or select reflects the program's *major* emphases. If you are a summative evaluator, you need to locate or construct the test that gives you the highest payoff in terms of assessing critical objectives. If you are a formative evaluator monitoring student progress over the course of the program, you might construct several specific tests to assess separately the development of the skills addressed by the different program units whose quality you want to monitor. On the other hand, much like a summative evaluator, you might construct one general test which could be given repeatedly to monitor overall progress in student achievement. If a program has few high priority objectives but still more than you feel you will be able to test, then consider sampling objectives.

Shrinking the set of objectives through ranking or sampling. Table 4 pages 28 and 29, gives a short description of four prioritization and sampling methods to consider as a means to deal with objectives when they are too numerous and/or when their relative importance to the program in question is unknown. Methods 1 and 2 both guide you in assigning priorities. Method 1 produces a list of objectives prioritized by means of one or another rating procedure. Rating can be based on either a "retrospective needs assessment" or an analysis of the relative emphases given to different objectives by the program *as implemented.* Retrospective needs assessment is a fancy term which means that concerned people—usually the evaluation's audience and program planners—are asked for their opinions about what the program should accomplish. Since these opinions are based on the raters' values and personal views toward the program's subject matter, objectives prioritization via this method usually results in measurements based on the program's ability to prepare students to function within a broader context—a higher grade, life, advanced math, a vocation, whatever. Rating based on the program-as-implemented, on the other hand, focuses the evaluation on how well the program is achieving whatever it seems to be trying hardest to accomplish. A test based on these objectives gives the program its best chance to show positive effects. Raters asked to examine objectives for program relevance should be, of course, as familiar with what the program *looks like in action* as possible.

To the extent that the program in operation addresses the objectives of its constituency and planners, the lists of important objectives produced by the two rating methods will coincide. Retrospective needs assessment and program implementation are presented separately, however, because the relative orderings of objectives produced by the two seldom do correspond.

Method 2 in Table 4 for reducing the size of a pool of objectives uses *objectives hierarchies*—logically derived learning sequences which point out key objectives.

Methods 3 and 4 use sampling. Following Method 3, you would take a simple random sample. Because of the importance of choosing the right objectives to guide *test selection,* Methods 1, 2, and 3 are discussed more fully in Chapter 3, pages 50 to 54.

Method 4, matrix sampling, is *not* a procedure for reducing the size of an objectives pool. Rather, it is a technique for testing *many* objectives by giving different sets of items to different groups of students. Each student does not, therefore, answer every question.[8]

Broadening the set of objectives by attending to generalization and transfer. Besides narrowing the pool of objectives underlying the test, consider expanding it. You might decide to look at objectives that reflect the development of skills *beyond those* specifically addressed by the program. Formulating objectives which describe skills somewhat peripheral to the program's focus or slightly in advance of those outlined by the program might help you demonstrate to the evaluation audience that the program has a relationship to students' learning *in the future* or *in related skill areas.* Such a specification of "generalization" or "transfer" objectives will help the staff and planners to justify the program as an integral part of students' educational careers.

What is more, a list of generalization and transfer objectives should broaden the criteria available to you for selecting a test. The rationale for this advantage goes something like this: selecting a test to measure program objectives demands that you match test items with expressed program objectives in the hope that you will find a test which is most congruent with your objectives and a minimum of items which test for knowledge extraneous to your objectives. If you have specified transfer and generalization objectives, you will be able to perform a more elaborate matching. You will be able to evaluate a given test not only for the information it provides about attainment of the primary objectives; you will also be able to assess the extent to which its items measure secondary objectives. The effect of this is simply to give you more information on which to base test selection.

In order to write generalization and transfer objectives, ask yourself or the program planners these questions:

- What skills will be learned *after* the program—skills for which the program supposedly will be preparing students?
- What particular abilities should we be developing in students that this program might be fostering indirectly?

8. Methods for using these and other procedures for prioritizing and sampling objectives and items can be found in Morris, L. L., & Fitz-Gibbon, C. T. How to deal with goals and objectives. In L. L. Morris (Ed.), *Program evaluation kit.* Beverly Hills: Sage Publications, 1978.

TABLE 4   Solutions to the

Method	Quick Summary	Advantages
1. Assigning priorities to all objectives through ratings	A group of approximately 15 raters rate all objectives according to a 5-point scale. Criteria determining ratings can vary. Mean ratings determine priorities.	• Yields accurate assessment of the priorities of interest groups represented by the raters. • Involves raters in the evaluation and is therefore likely to increase credibility. • Assures relevance of the evaluation to values and aims of the audiences, and/or to assessing effectiveness of the program *as implemented.*
2. Assigning priorities through objectives hierarchies	Objectives grouped into content areas, then charted from simple to complex. The more complex or "terminal" ones receive highest priority.	• Can be done by the evaluator alone–without cooperation from others. • Assigns priority to the most logically complex objectives, avoiding attention to too simple ones.
3. Sampling objectives	Objectives are randomly selected from the total set.	• Can be done by the evaluator alone–without cooperation from others. • The quickest, simplest method. • Treats all program objectives—on the test or not—as instructionally important.
4. Matrix sampling	Many items or objectives are used. They are assigned to parts of a test, and each part is given to different groups of students, usually randomly selected.	• Can be done by the evaluator alone–without cooperation from others. • Many items or objectives are tested, albeit with samples of students rather than all students. • Copying answers not a problem because students take different tests.

Problem of Too Many Objectives

Disadvantages	Recommendations
• Focuses evaluation on a small number of objectives. • Depends on cooperation of raters. • Time-consuming for evaluators and raters.	A good procedure to use, if you have time for it and can gain cooperation from enough raters. Especially recommended when it is deemed crucial that the evaluation show maximum sensitivity to the program as implemented, or to the wants or values of certain groups.
• Relatively time-consuming, depending on the number of objectives, • It may not be desirable to test only terminal, difficult objectives. • Subject matter may have no inherent hierarchy.	Probably should be used only when you as evaluator must narrow down the number of objectives yourself, without assistance, and when the subject matter lends itself to logical hierarchies.
• The risk exists of missing objectives or items that might be important thus reducing the credibility of the evaluation.	Highly recommended when all objectives are of about equal importance
• Somewhat involved procedure. • Data not entirely appropriate for use with some statistical tests. • Not practical for group administration with young children who must have the questions read aloud. • Not good for comparing students.	The only method by which you can assess *many* objectives or items. Due to the procedure's complexity, however, use it only when you cannot avoid testing many objectives or items.

- What other objectives might the school have for these students which could be more likely attained as a result of participation in this program?

Question 3. Can You Realistically Expect That the Achievement Objectives Will Have Been Accomplished by the Time You Plan To Do the Measuring?

Your answer to this question will determine the degree to which you focus on the processes—activities, materials—of the program in your evaluation in addition to its results or outcomes.

A program's objectives might be so complex or ephemeral that the program, as is, can only hope to *start* students toward attainment rather than fully accomplish the objectives within a specified time frame. For example, many advocates of open or humanistic education maintain that while students in open classrooms may not in any one semester appear to have learned more subject matter than students in more traditional classrooms, they actually have begun to learn how to solve problems, how to investigate areas of intellectual endeavor, and how to question and probe. In other words, their learning will eventually show a qualitative and therefore quantitative change; but such change may not be observable for quite some time.

Though your first impulse here—and it's not a bad one—might be to search for tests of creative problem solving, a drawback of such an approach is that probably neither you nor the program planners expect that a short exposure to the program will produce changes so substantial that they will show up on a general standardized test. If, as seems likely, you find no such change, how will you interpret the results? There are two solutions to consider in this situation: (1) Base the evaluation on more immediate and demonstrable objectives, and (2) augment the use of achievement tests with attention to the *processes* which the program has initiated for students.

The second solution bears some explanation. Though it is important in *any* evaluation to *describe* the program that students are experiencing, difficulty with adequately measuring the program's *outcomes* will make proper description of its materials, activities, and administration more important. This situation will require that you design a portion of the evaluation to determine whether the classroom instruction adequately reflects the *theory* upon which the program is based. The rationale for this shift in emphasis is a simple one. Money and effort have been invested in the program because people believe that the processes which it includes will bring about the development of the complex achievements reflected in its difficult-to-measure objectives.

In this situation, the best use of your time as evaluator will be to monitor whether the program looks and operates as it is supposed to. If you are a summative evaluator, you will tell the funding source whether it got what it paid for. If your function is primarily formative, then you will provide information for keeping the program on track. When you decide to focus on process, the questions you ask about the program will expand from, "Did the program promote the desired achievement?" to include "Did the program contain the materials and activities it was supposed to?" You should consult with your evaluation audience before deciding on such a course of action.

If you will be evaluating the program over a long period, say two or three years, an excellent idea is to collect information about changes in, say, creativity or self-direction and to note changes in the same group or across grade levels over time. After some time, you should start to see effects. In this case, it will become essential that you measure the complex objectives. By this time, the program can be looked upon as a test of whether the activities you have so carefully monitored do indeed bring about the desired achievements.

Question 4. Do You Have Available the Time and Resources To Custom-Make the Test?

In the best of all possible worlds, the way to assess the attainment of each achievement objective is to write for it valid items—five or more of them so that your measure is reliable—and administer a test made of these items to every student participating in the program. This will allow you to tell your audience about the degree of achievement of every objective. If you can match this ideal, then you are in a position to produce a highly credible assessment of program effects. Chapter 4 of this book, *Constructing a Test for Program Evaluation: A List of Resources,* will help you find sample objectives, test items, and item models. The chapter contains, as well, a list of How To . . . resources on the topic of test construction, focusing mainly on criterion-referenced testing since these seem most useful for program evaluation. Finally, the chapter lists test developers who offer to "do it all for you"—put together a test that will fit the program according to your specifications.

Custom-construction of a valid and reliable criterion-referenced test, however, is a task beyond the resources of many small-scale evaluations. In these cases, time, convenience, and your own concern for accurate measurement will dictate that you either purchase a test or use the results from one which is given as a matter of course. If you need to select a test, it is suggested that you use a formal procedure like the one outlined in Chapter 3 to compare tests. This standardized step-by-step procedure will ensure that you look at each test carefully, basing your choice on the match between its items and the objectives whose achievement you have decided to assess.

If you are a formative evaluator, your selection of a measurement instrument need not be so formal. Your task, in part, is to help determine the effectiveness of particular *subunits* of the program. For this job, you can use unit tests or tests created by the teachers of the program. You might even construct tests by sampling items from the students' practice exercises. Though you may want to use Chapter 2 and 3 to choose and evaluate the tests you will use, many of the problems of the summative evaluator when selecting a measurement instrument—selecting appropriate items for *general* learning and representing the overall effect of the program—might not concern you.

If you are a summative evaluator, you will first want to search out published tests which might be useful for your evaluation, since their measurement properties have been established. The introductory pages of Chapter 2 should help you find tests and order specimen sets. Then follow the program-test match procedure in Chapter 3 to help you assess the closeness of fit between the tests you have located and the program you are evaluating. If you can find no tests which seem appropriate, or if the test you select leaves you with a group of high priority objectives which will still not be assessed, you might then attempt to design a short criterion-referenced test of your own. Existing tests have the virtue of saving you time and allowing you to use materials which have already been field tested and should therefore be free of major problems. *A good rule of thumb is to use the best of what has already been developed instead of starting from scratch.*

Things To Remember

In summary, this chapter has called your attention to several matters pertinent to selecting or constructing an achievement test:

1. The need to consider how test data will be used.
2. The need to develop and clarify your achievement objectives before attempting to make decisions about how you will measure them.
3. The need to assure that the achievement objectives reflect the level of skill attainment that the program is intended to produce so that you will not find yourself evaluating a program aimed at high level concept attainment on the basis of whether it communicated simple vocabulary.
4. The need to decide on the relative importance of achievement objectives so that you will be able to focus on those of highest priority.
5. The need to determine whether achievement objectives are likely to be accomplished within the time frame of the evaluation so that you know whether to focus on outcomes or processes or perhaps both.

6. The need to decide how much of your achievement test will be selected from existing measures and how much you will construct yourself with the caveat that you should select existing measures whenever possible.

These reminders apply in practically any measurement situation. They can be summed up in one word: *relevance*. The measure you produce must focus on the same material as the program's instruction. Technical quality of the test as discussed in Chapter 5 only helps you to estimate the accuracy of whatever measures you choose. The first and most critical step in providing your evaluation with a good achievement measure is deciding *what* you want to measure.

For Further Reading

Lindvall, C. M., & Nitko, A. J. *Measuring pupil achievement and aptitude.* New York: Harcourt, Brace, Jovanovich, 1975.

Lyman, H. B. *Intelligence, aptitude and achievement testing.* Boston: Houghton Mifflin, 1968.

Mehrens, W. A., & Lehmann, I. J. *Standardized tests in education.* New York: Holt, Rinehart and Winston, 1969.

Chapter 2

Locating Existing Measures

The purpose of this chapter is to help you find an already published norm-referenced or criterion-referenced test. Chapter 1 mentioned the advantages of measuring achievement using already existing tests. Mainly, they save you time and give you the benefit of other people's experience. An instrument you buy or borrow has already been to some extent "debugged" and probably carries reliability and validity data. You might even be able to find results from its past administrations in other evaluation reports or in the test's accompanying manual. Observing proper caution, *you can compare these with your own.*

Finding Tests

Already written tests come from three sources:

1. The curriculum materials used for the program might be accompanied by pre- or posttests, unit tests or curriculum-embedded progress or mastery tests.
2. The state or district probably requires administration of a test (usually norm-referenced) in basic skills as part of its area-wide assessment program.
3. A test can be purchased from a test publisher or borrowed from a researcher, educational association, etc.

Any or all of these tests can be fit into your evaluation plans.

What To Do With the Tests That Come With the Program

Criterion-referenced tests are becoming increasingly popular for program management. Such tests, often "curriculum embedded," allow a student to proceed individually to later units on the basis of a passing score. Failing indicates a need for additional instruction. These tests are of great value to a formative evaluator. They help you to detect whether program instruction is of sufficient quality to allow students to master the program's own embedded test.

For summative evaluation, however, these tests are usually *not appropriate*. Because the tests are part of the program, their periodic passing does not guarantee that the program as a whole is accomplishing its objectives. The achievement test used for asessing the program's *overall effects* should be a different one—a norm- or criterion-referenced test purchased or constructed for that purpose and administered, usually as a posttest, to all or a representative sample of program participants. What is more, the *design* underlying your evaluation will prescribe certain times when tests should be administered. This schedule will seldom coincide with the times of administration of curriculum-embedded tests. Even a *time series* evaluation design requires that all students take tests at the same time, not when they are "ready."[9]

For the purposes of summative evaluation, the tests embedded in the curriculum *are* useful as *program implementation* information—evidence that the program occurred as planned. If you construct your *own* test for measuring overall program effects, tests embedded in the curriculum can be used as a source of suggestions for your test items.

A word should be said, in addition, about using the criterion-referenced pretest and posttest which accompany the program as a sole source of summative evaluation information. These tests have credibility problems. If you wish to use them, you will have to anticipate two questions from your audience:

1. *Is the pretest perhaps harder than the posttest?* Although not common, this could occur. This concern can be eliminated by reshuffling the items and retyping the forms. Use the odd-numbered items from both tests as *your* pretest and the even-numbered items as the posttest.

2. *Is the test giving the experimental group an undue advantage because of their greater familiarity with the format used in test items?* You can combat this problem by giving the control group, if there is one, practice with the same response formats, vocabulary, etc., to which the experimental group has been accustomed.

What To Do With a Test That Will Be Administered as a Matter of Course

If a test for state or district-wide assessment will be administered to most or all program students, then you should assess the appropriateness of *this*

---

9. Issues of design are discussed in several useful texts. See, for instance, Fitz-Gibbon, C. T., & Morris, L. L. How to design a program evaluation. In L. L. Morris (Ed.), *Program evaluation kit.* Beverly Hills: Sage Publications, 1978 and Campbell, D. T., & Stanley, J. C. *Experimental and quasi-experimental designs for research.* Chicago: Rand McNally, 1966.

test for your evaluation before you look for another. If the required test looks as though it could assess many of the major objectives of the program, you may have to look no further.

A procedure for determining the *match* between test items and program objectives, which begins on page 60, Chapter 3, can serve as a guide for evaluating any test you think might be used for the evaluation. If you decide to subject the required test to this scrutiny you might as well locate at least one *other* test to compare with the one you must use. The information you gain from this exercise will not only increase your knowledge of the technicalities of norm-referenced testing, it will help you to evaluate the relative quality and appropriateness of the test that you have been required to use.

Should you find that the required test compares poorly with the program's objectives you could supplement your measurements by giving a more relevant alternate test to a sample of students. You could also actively advocate a switch to another test. If none of this will work, and you are stuck with the required test, then one method remains for assuring a match between the test and the program: *extract information about how students performed on just those test items relevant to the program you are evaluating.* The procedure for extracting such information, though time-consuming, is straightforward:

1. Obtain a copy of the test that will be administered, and, if you can, cut up the test and paste each item on a separate card. Otherwise, have the items typed on cards.

2. Have someone who is familiar with the program sort the items into piles labeled

	MODERATELY	NOT
APPROPRIATE	APPROPRIATE	APPROPRIATE

3. Designate the items in the three groups "subtests." Make a list of item numbers for each subtest, and plan to analyze the three subtests separately when the test is scored.

4. Use as an indicator of program success *the mean score of all students in the program on the subtest composed of the most appropriate items.* Depending on the thoroughness of the score-reporting service you receive, this mean can be calculated in one of two ways:

   a. If time is short, or if the agency scoring the standardized test does not provide an item-by-item breakdown of students' scores, the relevant test items should be scored by hand *before* the tests are sent off for data processing. Add up item results for each student in the program on the relevant subtest, and from these scores compute the average score for program students.

b. If the agency scoring the test does provide a calculation, "percent correct" for program students on each test item, then you may save yourself some trouble by waiting for the printout. When it arrives, list this percent for each item in the subtest as a decimal (e.g., 83% becomes .83). Just add these decimals to obtain the average raw score of the students on the subtest.[10]

5. Similarly, obtain the mean score of program students on the other two subtests if you want some idea of what transfer of learning may have resulted from the program. That is, the program may have indirectly improved students' performance on items calling for skills somewhat related to the program, or even outside the primary focus of the program.

If you have available item results from the same test for students who are *not* receiving any instruction aimed at your program's goals, you should save such data for possible use in making comparisons of results on the three subtests.

If you have an evaluation design that seeks to compare the effectiveness of two programs in teaching goals that are common to both and if these

_____

10. Why does summing the decimals give you the average *raw* score? Because calculating the raw score from percents correct per item demands first dividing the sum of the percents by the number of items to get the average percent correct, and then multiplying again by this number to convert the average percent correct to a raw score. The operations of dividing and then multiplying by the same number cancel each other.

Consider this example. A test has *five* items. Percent of the students getting each item correct is as follows:

Item	Percent of students getting item correct	Translated to decimals
1	80%	.80
2	25%	.25
3	35%	.35
4	90%	.90
5	40%	.40
		2.70 = sum of decimals
		.54 = mean percent correct over five items

To determine the average raw score from the five items, you must multiply .54 by 5. You get 2.70 again.

goals are also addressed by items on the standardized achievement test used by your district, two changes in the procedure are called for:

1. The three piles for sorting items need to be re-labeled as, say:

APPROPRIATE FOR BOTH PROGRAMS	MODERATELY APPROPRIATE FOR BOTH PROGRAMS	REJECTED

2. Item results for students in different programs must be kept separate, so that mean subtest scores can be computed separately for students in different programs.

The procedure outlined here represents a fair way of using a standardized test to measure the achievement of some program objectives. In many cases, the amount of information it provides will be too incomplete to justify the time and effort involved.

Finding Published Tests

You will quickly discover that the majority of tests on the market are norm-referenced. This is because large-scale use of criterion methods for interpreting tests is relatively recent. Historically, tests have been used most often for comparing people. You will find, in fact, that unless the program focuses on achievement in such *basic skills* areas as elementary school reading and mathematics, you probably will be unable to locate a criterion-referenced test. If you want to test older students or focus on topics in the natural and social sciences, you will most likely need either to rely upon a norm-referenced test or develop a criterion-referenced test yourself. Chapter 4 provides resources to guide the latter process.

Published tests are almost always *standardized*. By the time they are placed on the market, these tests have completed a development phase during which they were validated on groups of subjects. When you purchase such measures, you will receive a *technical manual* that provides norms based on the scores of the tryout group, information about the validity and reliability of the instruments, and instructions for administering, scoring, and interpreting results. This information can often be obtained without commitment to buy the test if you write to the publishers requesting a *specimen set*. Most test publishers charge a small fee for specimen sets which usually consist of a sample copy of the instrument and an accompanying manual. A sample letter requesting specimen sets is provided in Figure 1.

The following section briefly describes several bibliographical sources that could be of use in your search for an existing achievement measure.

Copper Falls County School System
1400 Minocqua Drive
Ironwood, Michigan 49938
(412) 772-0047

January 8, 19XX

Gentlemen:

It has come to our attention that your instrument, (*The XYZ Reading Comprehension Test*), may be useful to us in evaluating the cognitive goals of our (*fourth grade reading program*).

Unless the specimen set costs more than (*$xx*), please send us one and bill us. This information should help us determine whether the test fits our needs. This means it should include data about the test's reliability and indicators of its validity.

If we decide to use (*The XYZ Reading Comprehension Test*), we will need information relevant to (*purchasing and scoring 80 copies*).

Thank you for your prompt attention to this matter.

Sincerely,

Figure 1. Sample letter requesting a specimen set

These compendia offer extensive lists of available tests. They name many more than could possibly be listed in this book.

Buros, O. K. (Ed.). *Mental measurements yearbooks.* Highland Park, New Jersey: Gryphon Press, 1938-1972 (seven volumes).

The 1972 edition of the MMY lists 2,967 tests, many of which are of interest to educators, and some of which are suitable for measuring student achievement. The book is available in the reference section of most college and large public libraries. Its primary intent is to provide information *and critical reviews* for *every* test that is commercially available in English-speaking countries and that is "published as a separate," that is, not just included somewhere within a journal or book. The critical reviews are "written by testing and subject specialists representing various viewpoints." A paragraph accompanying each test title tells you for whom the test is intended; what scores or ratings it yields; the titles of the subparts, if any; the different forms available; administration time; publishing source; and prices of materials.

The yearbooks also provide a list of new and revised books on testing, as well as references to articles discussing the quality or use of any test.

In 1975, Gryphon also published a series of derivative volumes, including the following: *Reading tests and reviews, Science tests and reviews, Social studies tests and reviews,* and *Vocational tests and reviews.* As these titles indicate, the books were compiled from appropriate sections of the *Mental measurements yearbooks,* and from *Tests in print II,* described below.

Buros, O. K. (Ed.). *Tests in print II.* Highland Park, New Jersey: Gryphon Press, 1974.

This volume differs from the MMY in several ways: it contains *no* critical reviews and *no* purchase prices, and it has a master index to the seven editions of MMY. Like the MMY, it describes tests in print by subject area. It points out as well, however, tests of that subject which have gone out of print. The major purpose of the 1974 edition of TIP is to provide an annotated listing of all known tests in print—2,467 of them—published as separates in English-speaking countries. Test descriptions, while primarily informational, also include some "statements implying criticism."

Hoepfner, R. et al. *The CSE test evaluation series.* Los Angeles: Center for the Study of Evaluation, UCLA Graduate School of Education, 1971-1976 (primarily subtitled by grade level).

This set lists commercially available tests of *student achievement and attitudes.* Tests are grouped according to the goals or subgoals they seem to measure, so the books are useful as test locators. The goals used for grouping tests are described in each book; they are organized into a taxonomy by subject (e.g., art, English) or by process (e.g., classifying, valuing). The tests, once keyed to these goals, were evaluated by raters who assigned points for suitability for the goal, convenience of administration, technical quality, and examinee appropriateness. These criteria are explained in the introduction to each book.

All tests reviewed are rated rather than described. The bulk of the text consists of tables reporting the numerical ratings, which are summarized as Good, Fair, or Poor. Tests intended for several grade levels frequently received better ratings for one level than for another. This series lists a large number of tests. The 1976 edition, dealing with elementary school tests, evaluates more than 800—and thousands of subtests. While the quality of most available instruments is low, judging from the ratings, the user is provided with a systematic means by which to compare the merits of many instruments that focus on similar educational goals.

While most of the tests evaluated in the series are norm-referenced, the latest volume, *CSE Criterion-Referenced Test Evaluations,* edited by C. B. Walker, is devoted exclusively to criterion-referenced tests.

Nafziger, D. H. et al. *Tests of functional adult literacy: an evaluation of currently available instruments.* Northwest Regional Educational Laboratory, Portland, Oregon, 1975.

This booklet reviews and evaluates 17 tests developed for *adults,* focusing on reading skills crucial for functioning in daily life. The book provides a rationale for the sorts of competencies required by each test. It describes as well the time and materials required, scoring procedures, and background information on each test's field testing, revision, or validation. The evaluation section consists of charts which rate each test on 33 criteria. Summary judgments of good, fair, or poor are made in four categories—measurement validity, examinee appropriateness, technical excellence, and administrative usability. The criteria used are explained in the text.

Tests that have subtests are evaluated at the subtest level. Thus, the book gives separate evaluations for vocabulary, reading comprehension, spelling, and oral reading. Tests are divided into three categories—those that are "very task oriented and immediately relevant to the examinee's everyday activities," those that are standardized, and those that are informal.

Sumner, R., & Robertson, T. S. *Criterion-referenced measurement and criterion-referenced tests.* Windsor, Berkshire, UK: National Foundation for Educational Research, 1977.

This book lists major articles on criterion-referenced measurement published between 1960 and 1975. Section 3 of the book contains articles describing criterion-referenced tests of foreign languages, mathematics, medical education, reading, science, and spelling. The book outlines, as well, two language arts tests, five math tests, and six reading tests, all attempting to meet the technical standards of criterion-referenced measurement. While many of the tests described are published in the U.K., some of them are published in the U.S.

Pletcher, B. P., Locks, N. A., Reynolds, D. F., & Sisson, B. G. *Guide to assessment instruments for limited-English-speaking students.* New York: Santillana, 1978.

As the introduction states, "the reviews contained in this catalogue are designed to be used by school personnel charged with locating and administering appropriate assessment instruments" to students whose first language is Chinese, French, Italian, Navajo, Portuguese, Spanish, or Tagalog, and whose command of English is limited. Each instrument reviewed was either developed or adapted for use with students in grades K-6. All instruments are available to the public and are presently in use somewhere in the U.S. None of the instruments included is bound to any particular set of curricular materials, and none is intended to identify developmental or constitutional deficiencies. Information given about each test includes its purpose, score interpretation, grade range, target ethnic group, conditions of administration, reliability and validity, manner of construction and revision, quality of norm scores, if any, and interpretability.

Accompanying each review is a critique of the test's cultural and linguistic appropriateness as judged by a geographically diverse group of educators who are native speakers of "the dialect spoken by the students for whom the instrument was intended."

Almost 100 instruments are reviewed for elementary school students whose first language is Spanish. Of these, 19 are measures of language dominance; 24, of proficiency in written or spoken Spanish; 17, of proficiency in English; 10, of achievement in more than one school subject; 6, of general ability or scholastic aptitude; and 12, of attitude or self-concept.

Twelve instruments are reviewed for use with elementary school students whose first language is Navajo, 11 for use with native speakers of French; 10 for Portuguese; 7 for Chinese; 5 for Tagalog, and 3 for Italian.

Young, M. B., & Schuh, R. G. *Evaluation and educational decision-making: A functional guide to evaluating career education.* Washington: Development Associates, for the U.S. Department of Health, Education, and Welfare, 1975.

The appendix of this booklet contains descriptions of nine instruments recommended by the authors and three "promising" instruments, all of which are relevant to career education either at the elementary or secondary level. Another instrument is described which receives mixed reviews.

Test descriptions include grade level, administration time, format, scoring, and cost. The book lists student outcomes relevant to career education and uses a table to match these with recommended or promising tests.

Lehman, P. R. *Tests and measurements in music.* Englewood Cliffs, New Jersey: Prentice-Hall, 1968.

This book contains descriptions and evaluations of published tests of music achievement and auditory and musical aptitudes as well as advice about constructing your own tests, and a discussion of measurement problems involved in measuring music appreciation and instrument performance. Ten published tests in the aptitude category, thirteen in the achievement category, and one test of band instrument performance are described and evaluated.

The appendix suggests further readings relevant to measuring musical achievement. Some deal with use and adaptation of commercially published music tests; others consist of journal articles containing tests that, according to the author, are well known but were never commercially published.

The following sources might contain tests of interest to you as well:

American Alliance for Health, Physical Education, and Recreation. *Testing for impaired, disabled, and handicapped individuals.* *[11] Washington: Author, 1976.

Fagan, W. T., Cooper, C. R., & Jensen, J. M. *Measures for research and evaluation in the English language arts.* * Urbana, Illinois: ERIC Clearinghouse on Reading and Communication Skills and National Council of Teachers of English, 1975.

Hunsicker, P., & Reiff, G. G. *Youth fitness test manual.* * Washington: American Alliance for Health, Physical Education, and Recreation, 1975.

Johnson, B. L., & Nelson, J. K. *Practical measurements for evaluation in physical education.* * Minneapolis, Minnesota: Burgess, 1974.

Mayer, V. J. *Unpublished evaluation instruments in science education: A handbook.* * Columbus, Ohio: ERIC/SMEAC Reference Center, Ohio State University, College of Education, 1974.

Peace, B. A. Appendix: Bibliography of social studies tests. In National Council for the Social Studies. *Thirty-fifth yearbook: Evaluation in social studies.* * Washington: Author, 1965, 230-248.

Suydam, M. N. *Unpublished instruments for evaluation in mathematics education: An annotated listing.* * Columbus, Ohio: ERIC Information Analysis Center for Science, Mathematics and Environmental Education, 1974.

Valette, R. M. Appendix: Commercial language tests. In *Modern language testing.* * New York: Harcourt Brace Jovanovich, 1977.

---

11. For a description of the contents of those publications that have been asterisked, see Chapter 4.

Selecting and Ordering a Test

Chapter 3 provides a detailed, highly prescriptive procedure for determining how well a test suits your particular program. You may decide on other, less formal ways of making your selection.

In any case, once you have chosen an achievement measure, the next step, of course, is to order it from the test publisher. Figure 2 shows a sample purchase order. The March 9 date on the purchase order was chosen for a reason. March is not too early in the year to order tests for May. You should allow at least two months for delivery so that you will have time in which to correct possible shipping errors. In addition, you should always give the publisher a shipping deadline that is well in advance of when you *must* have the test.

Copper Falls County School System 1400 Minocqua Drive Ironwood, Michigan 49938 (412) 772-0047			PURCHASE ORDER NUMBER № 128	

TO: _____ _____ _____	FROM: Marianne Howard _____ Title XIV Coordinator _____ _____

DATE ORDERED 3-9-XX	DATE NEEDED 4-15-XX	SHIP VIA Post	SPECIAL INSTRUCTIONS	

QUANTITY	DESCRIPTION	UNIT PRICE	AMOUNT
80	XYZ Reading Comprehension Test copies, Form ABC (CC 459)	.20	$16.00
100	XYZ Reading Comprehension Test answer sheets, Form ABC (CC 601)	.05	5.00
1	XYZ Reading Comprehension Test manual (CC 518)	.50	.50
2	XYZ Reading Comprehension Test scoring keys, Form ABC	.50	1.00

Figure 2. Sample purchase order

Determining How Well a Test Fits the Program

Before you select an achievement test, you should find out all you can about its development, procedures for administration, technical quality, and, if possible, the success of its previous use. If you are able to find an evaluation of the particular measure in the educational literature, perhaps in the *Mental Measurements Yearbooks* or the *CSE Test Evaluation Series* described on pages 40 and 41, you will have a good start toward test selection. If not, you will have to depend on the information provided by the publisher. Request a specimen set well before you will need the test—three or four months in advance. When sample measures arrive, look them over with a critical eye.

The test you use for assessing the achievement objectives of a program should be the one that allows you most confidently to make this statement: *There is a close fit between the items comprising the test and the major objectives of the program being evaluated.* The major criterion for test selection is relevance.

Determining relevance will require a *close examination of the items and procedures included on the test.* This chapter is intended to help you examine tests for their appropriateness to your program evaluation.

A word should be said, however, about the *timing* of the evaluation and your own potential influence on the shape of the program. The procedures described in this chapter assume that the objectives of the program are *fixed* and that the program was already underway when the evaluation began. This will almost certainly be the case if you are a summative evaluator and will characterize many formative situations as well. If you are in the fortunate position of starting the evaluation *before* the program has begun, though, you might be able to influence program content. If, during planning or initial implementation you were to locate a test closely related to the program and well suited to the students in question, then you could try to persuade planners *to develop the program with the test in mind.* This would assure you *in advance* that the program addressed the objectives of the test. Of course, the desirability of basing educational objectives on a test is a controversial issue. Some educators who lean toward humanism, for instance, deplore this as teaching to the test; and it is conceivable that such a practice, if improperly carried out, might narrow the curriculum to overemphasis on piecemeal skills. The suggestion, however, is not that objectives from the test form the sole basis for the curriculum. They should simply be included in curriculum planning. It is, unfair, after all, to expect students to perform well on a test whose objectives have not been addressed by their instruction, particularly if this test is one on which good scores are expected by the larger community which the school serves.

A Procedure For Locating an Appropriate Test

If the instructional content of the program has *already been established,* you will have to select the most relevant test. This chapter contains a 3-step process for judging test appropriateness. Its steps are outlined in Table 5.

Step 3, the last step in the process, describes how to use the *Table for Program Test Comparison* (TPTC) to arrive at numerical values—a Grand Average, Indices of Coverage and Relevance, and Number of Items per Objective. These tell you how well particular tests match the program's most important objectives. The TPTC, pages 58 and 59, has been adapted from a procedure suggested by the Center for the Study of Evaluation in the latest volume of *The CSE test evaluation series.*[12]

Although the procedure for determining test-program match outlined here is highly prescriptive, you might attend to the rationale on which it is based without following the procedure to the letter.

Step 1. Refine and Classify Objectives

Obtain the best description you can find of the program's achievement goals and objectives, or derive them from an outline of the curriculum covered by the program. Then revise these statements in consultation with the program staff until you have an agreed-upon list of program objectives. This list plays an important role in the test selection procedure, so make sure that it describes as specifically as possible what the program intends to achieve. The most helpful statement of an objective is one that depicts what a test item for that objective might look like. If you will be working from a curriculum outline, look through the instructional materials themselves to further clarify vaguely stated topics in the outline. Sometimes

---

12. The original procedure, formulated by L. Weinberger, appears in *CSE criterion-referenced test evaluations,* produced by C. B. Walker *et al. The CSE test evaluation series,* of which this is the latest volume, is described on page 41.

TABLE 5
Outline of Steps for Determining How Well a Test
Matches Your Program

Step 1. Refine and Classify Objectives*

A. Obtain a list of program objectives or an outline of curriculum topics and make sure they are stated as specifically as possible..
B. Then classify program objectives and select as many of them as you will be able to test. You may use one or more of the following methods:

1. Take a random sample if there are many objectives of about equal importance.
2. Have interested people from your audience rate or rank-order objectives. This increases the probability that the test or tests selected for the evaluation will be fair to the interests of the program's *constituency*. This is primarily a summative evaluation concern.
3. Have someone who knows the program's subject area organize program objectives into a skills hierarchy, and use it to help you decide which objectives it is most important to test. The objectives that should be emphasized in test selection are the more complex skills toward which the program builds, in the case of summative evaluation; whereas more attention to key enroute or component skills is needed for selection of tests for formative evaluation.
4. Have someone who knows the program sort objectives according to how closely they match the program *as implemented*.

Step 2. Obtain and Screen Test Specimens

A. Review the educational literature for critiques of relevant tests.
B. Obtain sample measures from publishers.
C. Screen the tests according to criteria you have decided upon.
D. Retain for consideration tests which meet the standards of the evaluation.

Step 3. For Each Test Under Consideration, Estimate the Relative Match of the Test Items to the Program Objectives from Step 1

A. Using the Table for Program-Test Comparison, number or code all test items and record these in column 1.
B. Number or code each program objective.
C. In column 2, record for each test item the program objective(s) addressed.
D. In column 3, record a value that reflects the importance of the objective.
E. In column 4, record a value (0, 1, or 2) for closeness of item content and format to the objective.
F. In column 5, record a value (0, 1, or 2) to reflect item appropriateness for the examinees.
G. In column 6 and 7 calculate the following:

- The product of the values in columns 3, 4, and 5.
- A Grand Average (sum of column 6 products ÷ number of items in column 1).
- Index of Coverage (total number of different objectives in column 2 ÷ total number of objectives).
- Index of Relevance (total number of non-zero products in column 6 ÷ total number of items in column 1).

---

*It is possible to choose a test according to its fit with the program *without* looking at explicit program objectives. Such a procedure, which is described on page 67, requires that people intimately familiar with the program perform a modified version of Step 3 only. This amounts to comparing tests by matching them to *implicit* program objectives.

statements of objectives will accompany published materials. Unfortunately, some publishers do a poor job of writing objectives to go with their materials, so you may find only a loose relationship between the objectives and the instructional activities for which the materials are designed. In that case, the publisher's objectives will be of little or no value to you.

Once you have a complete set of program objectives, you probably will want to shorten the list. In using the TPTC to compare the relevance of tests, 30 to 50 objectives is a manageable number. Depending on the rating method you use, you might be able to reduce the size of the set of objectives and rate them at the same time.

Reducing the Set and Rating Objectives for Importance[13]

The procedures for reducing the size of a set of objectives outlined in this section were briefly described in Table 4, page 28. You may want to check the table for a review of the advantages and disadvantages of each method. It is also possible to use some combination of these methods.

Take a random sample

The quickest way to narrow down the number of objectives is to choose some at random from the larger pool. If the selection of a test used for the evaluation will be based upon a random sample of objectives, then *all* objectives have been treated as being of equal importance, since the items from any objective could appear on the test. If teachers do not know at the outset of the program which of the program objectives will be tested, they are less likely to narrow the focus of the program to only those objectives that will be measured.

Simple random sampling, however, might expose your test results to the criticism, "You didn't test for the most important skill we wanted the students to learn." You can avoid this situation by having members of your evaluation audience or the staff add to the random sample a few more of what they consider to be the *more critical* objectives.

Have interested members of your audience rate objectives

Rating of objectives by members of the program's constituency assists you in choosing a test that reflects the objectives most important to the people who want an assessment of the program. Such a procedure, which could be

    13. Step-by-step guidance in sampling objectives and rating according to audience preferences and objectives hierarchies is contained in Morris, L. L., & Fitz-Gibbon, C. T. How to deal with goals and objectives. In L. L. Morris (Ed.), *Program evaluation kit*. Beverly Hills: Sage Publications, 1978.

called a *retrospective needs assessment,*[14] is particularly useful for summative evaluation.

If you decide to ask people to rate objectives, choose a set of raters—teachers, parents, students, school board members, curriculum experts, district administrators—who represent the viewpoints of the program's constituency. The number of raters is up to you. Ask the raters to examine the pool of objectives and then sort them into categories with point values:

1 points   Unimportant
2 points   Below average importance
3 points   Average importance
4 points   Above average importance
5 points   Very important, critical, or essential

Instruct the raters to base their decisions on what *they* think the students should learn from the program. Collect the ratings or rankings and compute a mean per objective for the whole set of raters. If raters' opinions tend to polarize, you will have to calculate mean ratings to represent the views of the different interest groups. The 30 to 50 highest ranking objectives (or whatever number you are prepared to test) would then be used as the basis for choosing the test.

Have someone who knows the subject area construct a skills hierarchy

A hierarchy reflects the order in which skills are presumably learned. A test based on objectives rated in this way will contain a greater proportion of items which measure achievement of the "terminal" objectives toward which the program builds, and fewer of the "enroute" skills whose presence can be inferred from mastery of the more advanced objectives.

Usually hierarchies are constructed by first sorting objectives into three categories: simple, intermediate, and complex or terminal objectives. Then graphs, like the one in Figure 3, page 50, are constructed, showing interrelationships—that is, which objectives must be mastered in order to learn the others. Highest priority is usually given to those objectives which represent ultimate program goals and to those objectives, such as objective 1 in Figure 3, which feed into more than one subsequent objective.

---

14. A needs assessment is an announcement of educational needs as expressed in the school curriculum and in school policies by representatives of the school or district constituency. The rating procedure described here is the most commonly used method for gathering community opinion about priorities placed on objectives.

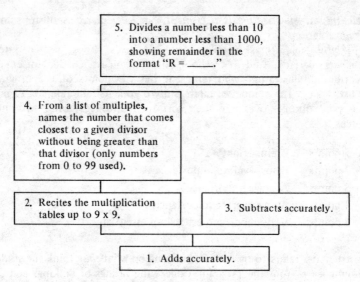

Figure 3. Portion of long division skill hierarchy

Have someone who knows the program sort objectives according to how closely they match the program as implemented

The best test on which to base decisions about modifications in a program is one that measures the effectiveness of what the program is actually trying hardest to do. A test reflecting the objectives of the program as implemented is indispensible for formative evaluation. For summative evaluation, such a test is a fair basis for judgment of program effectiveness. It holds the staff accountable for accomplishing what they actually attempted.

In order to rate objectives according to the extent to which they reflect the program in operation, you will need one or two people who have seen the program in action and have carefully examined the curriculum. Have them classify objectives into four categories:

a. Those that appear in "**O**fficial" program statements and which have also been **I**mplemented (**O-I** objectives)

b. **O**fficial objectives which are **N**ot reflected in program implementation (**O-N**)

c. Other objectives, possibly achieved through **T**ransfer or **G**eneralization from the program (**T-G**)

d. **U**nmentioned objectives—*not* officially stated, but underlying the program as **I**mplemented (**U-I**)

O-I Objectives. Objectives which are listed in the program proposal, plan, or curriculum outline, and which have received considerable attention as the program takes place at *nearly all its sites* should be given highest priority when a test is selected. These are important to everyone.

O-N Objectives. Objectives which were announced but which the program's instruction did not address should *not* be reflected in the test. They may have been originally included to make the program more appealing to the funding source or to round out a portrayal of the program's comprehensiveness. More often than not, neglected objectives are a sign that the ambitions of program planners simply exceeded what teachers could realistically be expected to carry out.

T-G Objectives. These are stated objectives which fit into neither of the first two categories. They are typically generalization and transfer skills which students in the program *might* develop in connection with their instruction but which are not expressly addressed by the program activities. T-G objectives *are* relevant to program activities and therefore do not belong to the O-N category. On the other hand, it would be unfair to hold the program accountable for their achievement since they are peripheral to the program's focus. Test selection should lean a little toward these objectives, but not too far.

U-I Objectives. It is possible that the program as implemented—*at least at some of its sites*—strives toward objectives which have not been mentioned in official documents and which do not appear in your original list. Request that whoever classifies the O-I, O-N, and T-G objectives take some time to search out achievement ambitions of the program staff that have gone unrecorded. A program may have acquired these additional objectives in any number of ways. Some might represent prerequisite skills which were added because of deficiencies in the learning of entering students. Others probably just evolved, whether because of student interests, teacher judgments, or special opportunities for learning that arose during the program. Whatever the reason for their appearance, the program gives them some attention, so they should also be part of what the test measures.

Classifying objectives—by ratings, hierarchies, or degree of implementation—gives you information that can help you to select tests. Not only can you make a general judgment about the test's appropriateness to the program objectives, you can also select different tests on the basis of which *kind* of objectives they address. In addition, your classification can be useful to you when all the data are in and you must interpret test results for your report.

Classifying objectives can also be an important way of involving as many interested people as you can in the evaluation process. You should, of course, report back to them the resulting classification as a picture of your perception of the program's goals. If you are a formative evaluator, such information should be flowing back and forth anyway. If you are a summative evaluator, this communication can help you and your audience to arrive at a common understanding of the program's aims. Such conversations contribute to the credibility of the evaluation.

Step 2. Obtain and Screen Test Specimens

Completing the Table for Program-Test Comparison (TPTC) requires effort. You will therefore want to limit this rigorous examination to the few tests that you are considering seriously. Before you sit down with the table, therefore, you should *screen* the test specimens you have located.

Your *criteria* for screening tests will depend on your situation. They will reflect the demands you or your audience intend to make of the test concerning, for instance, types of scores provided, test length, or technical quality. To examine your thinking about major test features, complete the short questionnaire in Table 6, pages 56 and 57.

Then eliminate tests which omit the features that are most important to you.

Step 3. For Each Test Under Consideration, Estimate the Relative Match of the Test Items to the Program Objectives from Step 1

Table 7, the Table for Program-Test Comparison (TPTC), pages 58 and 59, is designed to help you perform a detailed analysis of the relevance of a test for systematically measuring the outcomes of the program. Using the TPTC involves one-by-one comparison of each of the test's items with the most important objectives of the program being evaluated. The method has several advantages over informal assessments of this match:

1. It is systematic. The procedure can be explained to people, used over and over with different tests, and modified to suit your situation.
2. The step-by-step procedure calls attention to characteristics of a test that should determine test selection in any situation. It helps you to compute separately:

    • The *Grand Average*—a general index of the relative appropriateness of the test for measuring the program's highest priority objectives with your particular target group of students. A high Grand Average means that the test contains a large proportion of items addressed to the program's most important objectives.
    • The proportion of items on the test that are relevant to the program—the *Index of Relevance*.
    • The proportion of the objectives of the program covered by the test—the *Index of Coverage*.
    • The number of test items per program objective.

3. Because there are so many judgments to make, the procedure uses *numerical ratings* to represent test characteristics. This enables you to aggregate judgments into the indices just described. The indices then give you an easy method for comparing tests.

For your convenience, Appendix A contains a larger Table for Program-Test Comparison that can be photocopied. A step-by-step description of how to fill in the table begins on page 60 and continues through page 68.

How To Complete the Table for Program-Test Comparison (TPTC)

The TPTC has seven columns for recording the results of each step in the process of matching test items with program objectives. In column 1, you are asked to list the numbers of the test items. Column 2 calls for you to find and note which of the program's objectives best matches each item. Completing each remaining step requires that you *assign points* showing the importance or appropriateness of the items and objectives. Column 3 records your judgment of the *importance to the program of the objectives the item measures.* In column 4, you write down your judgment of the *appropriateness of the item's format and content* for measuring the objective. Column 5 records the item's appropriateness to the students in question. Once columns 3 through 5 have been filled in, the numbers you have recorded are multiplied. Their product is noted in column 6. Data from these columns are then used to compute indices of coverage and relevance to help you to decide which test is best for measuring the particular objectives of the program.

Before you begin filling out the table, assemble specimens of the tests you plan to examine and a list of program objectives arranged according to their priority. *Be sure that each test item and written objective is numbered* or has been assigned some letter/number code which can be entered into columns 1 and 2.

Precisely *who* fills out the TPTC depends on circumstances. Armed with prioritized objectives, you can probably do a fairly effective job yourself. A good way to reduce the effects of rater errors and idosyncracies is for you to adjudicate the judgments of *two or three raters* or average the indices they obtain. People working with the TPTC should practically know the objectives by heart. They will need to remember relevant objectives when they read the test items.

Completing the TPTC requires following this step-by-step procedure:

Fill in identifying information

Supply relevant information at the top of the table—the test name and level, the subject matter area, the grade level of students for whom the

TABLE 6
Test Selectors' Screening Questionnaire[15]

How important is each of the following factors to you or your audience in choosing an achievement test?

Circle a number for each:

Feature	Importance Rating				
	barely		moderately		crucially
1. The age or grade levels for which the test is intended	1	2	3	4	5
2. Whether "cultural bias" has been minimized	1	2	3	4	5
3. How long the test or selected sub-test takes to administer	1	2	3	4	5
4. Whether the test has undergone field tryouts	1	2	3	4	5
5. The sorts of scores provided—raw scores only, percentiles, stanines, mastery cut-offs per objective	1	2	3	4	5
6. Whether the test items* are explicitly keyed to specific skills or objectives	1	2	3	4	5
7. How precisely test objectives or skills have been described	1	2	3	4	5
8. Whether there is more than one item for each objective measured	1	2	3	4	5
9. Whether the students in the field test and norm sample are a national cross-section	1	2	3	4	5
10. Whether the students in the field test and norm sample are comparable to your students	1	2	3	4	5

*Appendix B lists some more specific questions you might ask about item quality.

15. Adapted from Dotseth, M., Hunter, R., & Walker, C. B. Survey of test selectors' concerns and the test selection process. *CSE Report No. 107.* Los Angeles: Center for the Study of Evaluation, UCLA Graduate School of Education, 1978.

Table 6 (continued)

Feature	Importance Rating				
	barely		moderately		crucially
11. Whether the written materials and instructions are appropriate both in terms of clarity and appeal, for the students in your program	1	2	3	4	5
12. Whether the test has alternate forms	1	2	3	4	5
13. Clarity of the instructions to the examiner	1	2	3	4	5
14. Whether test items are indexed to various textbooks or curricular materials for prescriptive purposes	1	2	3	4	5
15. Whether validity data are adequate and favorable	1	2	3	4	5
16. Whether reliability data are adequate and favorable	1	2	3	4	5
17. How well the test scores differentiate among low achievers	1	2	3	4	5
18. How well the test scores differentiate among high achievers	1	2	3	4	5
19. How credible and useful the publisher's instructions are on using scores for judging students' mastery or non-mastery	1	2	3	4	5
20. How easy it is for students to record their answers	1	2	3	4	5
21. The ease and objectivity of scoring	1	2	3	4	5
22. Whether a record keeping system is provided for classroom use in individualized instruction	1	2	3	4	5

TABLE 7   Table for

Test_____   Subject area_____

Type: ☐ CRT ☐ NRT ☐ Unclear   Test level_____

                                   Grade level_____

1 Test item	2 Objectives that match item	3 Importance of objective					4 Item content and format analysis		
		1	2	3	4	5	0	1	2

box B

Total # of items on the test

box C

of *different* objectives listed

Program-Test Comparison (TPTC)

Rated by _____

Date _____

box A	Total # of program objectives used for selection

5			6	7
Item appropriateness for students			Product of columns 3, 4, and 5	
0	1	2		Summary figures

Grand Average

Grand Tally (box D) ÷ total # of items on the test (box B) =

Index of Coverage

# of objectives listed in column 2 (box C) ÷ total # of program objectives (box A) =

Index of Relevance

# of products in column 6 (box E) ÷ total # of items on the test (box B) =

box D	Grand Tally

box E	# of products in column 6 > 0

publisher says the test is most appropriate, whether the test is norm-(NRT) or criterion-referenced (CRT), the rater's name, and the date. In box A, fill in the total number of objectives used for test selection.

Column 1: List the test items

Since you will complete the table with the test in front of you, you need only enter in column 1 a numerical identifier for each test item. If the items on the test are numbered—simply 1 through, say, 50—then write these down. Otherwise, use a numerical or letter-number code of your own to distinctively identify items. If the test you are evaluating has quite a few items, you will have to make several copies of the table.

Be sure when completing this step to list the test's *items*, not its *objectives*—even if the test has been based on objectives which the publisher has provided. Test publishers have begun to include statements of objectives with published tests—normed as well as criterion-referenced. The objectives often appear in the test's manual, and in some tests they are actually written on the test form. *If the test's items are available, it is inappropriate to use the announced objectives of the test as your indication of what the test measures.* It is the *items*, after all, that the examinees will encounter, regardless of the objectives written by the test publisher. And these items will be used to measure attainment of *the program's* objectives. The publisher's objectives need not enter into your decision about test appropriateness at all. For this reason, you would do well to either ignore the objectives which accompany the test, or use them as a basis for *initial* screening.

Now fill in columns 2 through 5 for each item, *working across the page rather than down the columns.* A straight edge or a ruler will help you keep your place.

Columns 2 and 3: Find the objective that best matches the item and record its importance rating

To complete column 2, match your list of objectives with each of the test items. Decide which program objective, if any, the item seems to measure, and write down the objective's number or code name. This task will be relatively easy if the objectives are fresh in your memory and you understand them well. Then *double check* the list of objectives to ensure that your matches make sense and to look for objectives you may have forgotten. Note that *the objective and item need not match exactly.* If you are in doubt about whether an item and/or objective match, decide that they *do.* The *degree of match* can be more precisely assessed later when you complete column 4. What is important here is to record the objectives which are addressed *at all* by the test, even peripherally.

It may occur to you that an item seems to assess *more than one* objective. You should list in column 2 *every* objective the item seems to address. But because completing columns 3, 4, and 5 with multiple objectives per item will be too complex, you will need to choose *one* of the objectives to use as a reference when filling in columns 3, 4, and 5. Which objective you choose is up to you, but you will probably want to select the one the item seems to assess most closely, and circle the entry for that objective.

While completing the TPTC you should notice that the test contains several similar items addressed to the same objective. In most cases, this is a desirable test feature. To avoid repeating test analysis every time a similar item occurs, simply copy across columns the information from the first occurrence of an item of a particular type.

Filling in column 2 equips you eventually to determine two other important characteristics of the test: the number of items referencing each objective, and the objectives which are and are not covered by the test. These are determined after the table has been completed.

If the item in column 1 seems to measure *no objective* of the program, then write "none" in column 2, and *draw a horizontal line all the way across the table to show that you need not consider that particular item again.* If you find that this exercise has eliminated more than a quarter of the test items from consideration, then think about declaring the test irrelevant to the program.

While you are completing column 2, also fill in column 3. The numerals entered into column 3 are *points* given each objective entered or circled in column 2 to reflect its relative importance.

Column 3 has space for assigning up to 5 points. You need not, however, use this wide a range. To complete column 3 write down the numbers of points assigned to the objective in the appropriate space, as in Figure 4, page 62.

How you complete column 3 depends on which method you used to select and prioritize objectives (pages 50 to 54). If you *sampled objectives* randomly, or if for any reason they have not been prioritized, then ignore column 3. If your sample contains some objectives of higher priority than the others, you could assign them 2 or 3 points by asking: Are they 2 or 3 times more important? Other objectives in the sample should receive one point.

If interested members of the program's constituency ranked or rated objectives, then enter in column 3 the average number of points assigned or the relative rank of the objective. As you will remember, a 5-point rating scale was suggested for this procedure.

If a *skills hierarchy* determined priority, points can be assigned objectives according to their relative importance for mastering the subject area. Since a 5-point range probably demands too fine a discrimination among objectives rated by this method, assign 1, 2, or 3 points. Give 3 points to terminal objectives toward which much of the curriculum builds, and to intermediate objectives which are prerequisite to a large number of other objectives. Give 2 points to other terminal objectives and less crucial intermediates, and 1 point to any other objectives.

If objectives were classified according to the degree to which they underlie the program *as implemented,* then use a 3-point range: Assign O-I and U-I objectives 3 points; give T-G objectives 2 points and O-N, 1 point.

You could, as well, combine results from the different prioritizing procedures. How you assign points in column 3 and how many you assign are up to you—*as long as your procedure remains consistent throughout the whole test-program match exercise.*

The point values entered into column 3, you will note, *weight* the indices toward tests that contain items measuring the most important program objectives.

Using columns 4 and 5, you will examine the appropriateness of item content and format for measuring the objectives and for administration to

Figure 4. Filling in the Table for Program-Test Comparison (TPTC)

the student group in question. Items which receive high ratings in column 3 because they are associated with important objectives can be *promoted*, so to speak, if they again receive high ratings in columns 4 and 5 for *degree of match* with the objectives and students. On the other hand, these items can be demoted if they receive low ratings.

Column 4: Match the content and format of item and objective

When completing column 2, you listed objectives from the program that seemed to be related to test items, disregarding somewhat the closeness of this relationship. Column 4 asks that you make a more precise decision about how closely the item and objective match. This decision is based on an analysis of the test item's *content and format.*

Content analysis means looking for overlap between the knowledge or performance required by the test and the program ambitions stated by the objective. This analysis is critical if you are to ensure finding a valid measure of the program's effectiveness. You can determine this overlap by asking yourself, for each item, the following sorts of questions:

- What specific *learning* does the item seem to measure? What specific math skills, for instance, or what grade level in reading? What kinds of topics are covered in the reading section: scientific, biographical, fiction? Is the *vocabulary* used in the test items similar to that used in the program?
- Is the item something the student might actually have encountered during the course of the program? Are these the sorts of equations used in performing calculations? Does the unit on invertebrates, for instance, mention this particular principle? Do the reading exercises cover this sort of subject matter?

Column 4 allows you to enter either a 0, a 1, or a 2. These point values represent a continuum of match between the item and the objective. A good strategy is to first classify the objective's *content,* giving it a tentative rating of 0, 1, or 2, before analyzing its format. Assume, first, that the content match between item and objective is so-so, and give the item a rating of 1. If the match seems particularly apt, then promote the rating to 2. If you have serious doubts about the appropriateness of the fit, and perhaps even about your decision in column 2 that the objective matches the item at all, then assign a zero. If item content matches *no other* objective, then stop considering the item altogether.

After you have analyzed content, move on to a consideration of *format.* The critical question in examining a test for *appropriateness of format* is this: *Do item formats on the test correspond to those that are learned by the students in the program*? If the test is to be valid for your purposes, they should. A format that is new to a student might prevent her from demonstrating knowledge that she indeed has. A student, for example, who is accustomed to vertical presentations for adding fractions,

for example, $\begin{array}{r} \frac{1}{2} \\ + \frac{1}{4} \\ \hline \end{array}$ might be confused by a problem on the test that is

arranged $\frac{1}{2} + \frac{1}{4} =$ _____. Though she knows how to add fractions, the format may trip her up. Too much format interference of this sort will invalidate the test.

A classic place where format interference can occur is in the spelling tests that require the student to select a misspelled word from a list, rather than write the word from dictation. If the student's experiences in the spelling program have revolved around dictation, then the test format might cause her to commit errors when dealing with words that she can indeed spell. Although it has not been conclusively demonstrated that such format changes do indeed bias test results, the danger is always there.

It is quite likely that you will find *some* format differences between the presentation of items on the test and the experiences of students in the program. *If you think that format differences will not seriously affect test results, then let the numeral you chose to represent the match between test content and program objectives represent your opinion.* Enter this quantity in column 4. On the other hand, if you think that format differences might seriously affect student performance on this item, then reduce your rating of the match between the item and the objective accordingly, and record this numeral instead.

If you find that you have had to enter a zero in column 4 because of content or format mismatch, then draw a horizontal line through that row of the table. Entering a zero in any column will cause the eventual row product to equal zero.

In summary, a good strategy for arriving at a numerical value for column 4 is to assume first that the match between item and objective is so-so, allowing the rating to be 1. If you have doubts about the appropriateness of fit between either content or format, then reduce your rating to zero. On the other hand, if the item seems to fit the objective well, then increase your rating to 2.

Column 5: Rate the item's appropriateness for the program's target group

Even if the content and format of an item appear to match an important objective, it is still possible that the wording or amount of previous experience assumed by the item makes it inappropriate for the developmental level, ethnic background, etc., of the student group who are to be tested. Column 5 allows you to make a quick assessment of the item, assigning 0, 1, 2 points to denote appropriateness for the test takers. Appropriateness is often just a matter of whether the item is too easy or too hard for the group. Information in the test manual about difficulty indices per item might aid this decision. Again, a good strategy for completing column 5 is to first assume that the item is appropriate enough to deserve a rating of 1. If, however, the item seems just too easy or too hard, assign a rating of zero; if it is highly appropriate or just about perfect, promote the rating to a 2.

Column 6: Combine judgments for each item

Multiply the numbers in columns 3, 4, and 5. Enter this product in column 6.

The test you are examining might be a criterion-referenced test which allows you to administer subtests of your own choosing and eliminate others. If this is the case, then *weed out* subtests whose absence will increase the test's relevance to the program *before* you go on to column 7 and calculate indices for test choice.

Column 7: Complete the summary figures and indices

Column 7 lists equations for calculating three indices for each test so that you can compare the appropriateness of different tests for measuring program objectives. These three indices are:

1. *The Grand Average.* This is computed by adding the products in column 6 to produce a Grand Tally, and then dividing the Grand Tally by the total number of test items listed in column 1. The Grand Average is the best summary index for deciding which of the tests you have analyzed is most appropriate to the program. *The test with the largest Grand Average covers your most important objectives most adequately.* Note, however, that this is a *relative* judgment: *better than* the other tests does not mean *adequate.* A test with a high Grand Average might still leave important objectives unmeasured. The extent to which this has occurred can be estimated from the Index of Coverage.

   You might also want to compare the Grand Average you have obtained with the maximum possible. If *all* the tests you examine score too low you might decide not to use any of them. The maximum Grand Average possible in each of your test analysis exercises will equal

$$\frac{\text{the maximum number of points in}}{\text{column 3 possible per objective}} \times 4$$

   The smallest value that the Grand Average can assume is, of course, zero.

2. *An Index of Coverage.* Coverage—the extent to which the test *covers* program objectives—equals the proportion of program objectives measured by the test. To compute the Index, first count the number of *different* objectives listed in column 2. *If some items were found to be*

relevant to two or more objectives, count all of them. If a row of entries was crossed out because a zero rating occurred in columns 4 or 5, *do not* count the objective mentioned in that row. Enter the sum of the different objectives covered in box C below column 2; then divide this number by the total number of objectives on your initial list, the quantity in box A.

The maximum possible Index of Coverage is 1; the minimum, 0. In cases where the Index of Coverage is high, say .75 or better, you can feel secure that the test represents the program fairly—particularly if the test ranks well according to other indices. If the Index is low, then find out *which* objectives the test covers and omits. It probably concentrates on a certain *category* of skills ignoring others. If this is so, then you know where the test is deficient, and you might be able to choose two tests which, combined, cover a larger set of program objectives. You could, as well, *construct* a test to measure the objectives left out and/or those which are poorly measured by the test you are thinking of selecting. You can get an idea of which objectives are measured poorly by looking at the fourth index, Number of Items per Objective, described below.

3. *An Index of Relevance.* This index tells you what proportion *of the test* fits your set of objectives, and conversely, how much of the test is *irrelevant* to your evaluation. To compute the Index of Relevance, first count *the number of products* in column 6 that *do not equal zero* and enter this quantity in box E below that column. Then divide by the total number of items on the test. The Index of Relevance will have a value between zero and 1; it tells you about what proportion of the time students taking the test will actually be working on tasks relevant to program objectives. The logical opposite of this measure, of course, is the proportion of time students will spend displaying skills that have nothing to do with program instruction.

In addition to the three indices in column 7, the TPTC allows you to compute a set of values that will be important if you intend to interpret test results objective-by-objective:

The Number of Items per Objective. You can determine this by looking at column 2, and counting how many times each particular objective is mentioned. The reliability of a test is strongly related to the number of items the test contains. A reliable test of a single objective should contain at least three and ideally five items. If you note only two items per objective, the test can squeak by. If you notice that only one or two items cover each objective, the test might still allow you to make *summary statements about the program in general*; but you will be unable to say anything about achievement of any *particular* objective.

How To Use the Table for Program-Test Comparison Without Program Objectives

In the absence of clearly written objectives, you can adapt the TPTC procedure and choose a test based on how well the program's *staff* feels the test fits the *program*. This amounts to asking people who know the program well to evaluate the test according to their implicit notions of the program's aims. To do this, augment the standard procedure in the following way:

- List test items in column 1 of the TPTC as the test selection procedure recommends, and cross out column 2.
- Give the candidate tests and the TPTC to a few people who are intimate with the program, and have them begin test examination at column 3. Ask the staff members to assign a 1-to-5 rating to each item according to the importance of the skill it measures to the overall program.
- Have the raters complete columns 4, 5, and 6 as prescribed.
- In column 7, compute the Grand Average and Index of Relevance. Because you are without a pool of explicit objectives, you will be unable to compute an Index of Coverage. You will *not* be able to count the number of test items per objective, the fourth index of interest.
- Have the group of raters give you an informal Index of Coverage by estimating the proportion of the program the test does seem to cover and by listing program areas it fails to touch on at all.

Then choose a test

In many cases, the test most useful for your evaluation will be the one with the largest Grand Average, particularly if this average is close to the maximum possible. It will come closest to measuring the program's most important objectives. Be careful, however, to temper your choice based on the Grand Average with a look at the other indices.

Regardless of the size of the Grand Average, you probably should not use a test that has an Index of Coverage lower than about .65, unless you can test in some other way for achievement of the objectives the test omits. On the other hand, a test with a very high Grand Average and a low Index of Coverage probably omits mainly lower priority objectives. In this case, you may decide to just ignore those objectives.

A test with a comparatively high Grand Average will rarely show a low Index of Relevance. If this does happen, it means that a small part of the test is doing a good job of measuring some important program objectives. The Grand Average has been inflated by their high ratings in column 3. Unless you will be able to extract and administer only those items that are relevant to the program, such a test is probably not suitable for evaluating it.

The Number of Items per Objective is an important index to consider *if you intend to interpret the test's results objective-by-objective*. In general, you will be able to announce with confidence that students have achieved particular objectives only if the test contains four or five items per objective. What is more, when you interpret results for each objective, the items should be fairly homogeneous and close to the objectives in content and format (the concern of column 4). Regardless of other indices, a test that allots each objective only 1, 2, or 3 items may not give you a reliable indication of their achievement.

On the other hand, if you plan to use the score from the whole test to reflect general program achievement, then the Number of Items per Objective will carry less weight in influencing your choice. In this case, you should use your information about which objectives are addressed by which proportion of test items to assure that the test as a whole gives strong emphasis to important objectives and minor emphasis to less important ones. This is the issue of content validity, described on pages 96 to 101.

For Further Reading

American Psychological Association, American Educational Research Association, and National Council on Measurement in Education. *Standards for educational and psychological tests and manuals.* Washington, D.C.: American Psychological Association, 1974.

Armbruster, B. B., Stevens, R. J., & Rosenshire B. Analyzing content coverage and emphasis: A study of three curricula and two tests. *Technical Report No. 26.* Urbana, Illinois: Center for the Study of Reading, University of Illinois, 1977.

Dotseth, M., Hunter, R., & Walker, C. B. Survey of test selectors' concerns and the test selection process. *CSE Report No. 107.* Los Angeles: Center for the Study of Evaluation, UCLA Graduate School of Education, 1978.

Hambleton, R. K., & Eignor, D. Guidelines for evaluating criterion-referenced tests and test manuals. *Journal of Educational Measurement,* 1978, *15*(2).

Jenkins, J. R., & Pany, D. Curriculum biases in reading achievement tests. *Technical Report No. 16.* Urbana Illinois: Center for the study of Reading, University of Illinois, 1976.

Katz, M. *Selecting an achievement test.* Princeton, New Jersey: Educational Testing Service, 1973.

On the topic of sampling . . .

Fitz-Gibbon, C. T., & Morris, L. L. How to design a program evaluation (Chapter 8: How to randomize). In L. L. Morris (Ed.), *Program evaluation kit.* Beverly Hills: Sage Publications, 1978.

Chapter 4

Constructing a Test for Program Evaluation: A List of Resources

Even if you decide to construct your own achievement test, suited to the particulars of the program you are evaluating, it is important to take advantage of the experience of others. You should try to become familiar with the do's and don'ts accumulated by educators who have designed tests over the years. When you choose which objectives to measure and what types of items to use, you should know something about the alternatives you have rejected so that you can justify your measurement plan. When possible, you should build the test from existing objectives, items, and even subtests—particularly if you have evidence of their quality. In short, you should try not to reinvent the wheel.

An abundance of advice is available to you in books and journals on the topics of constructing tests and describing student achievement. Therefore, rather than provide yet another "how to" introduction to test construction, this chapter lists a variety of existing resources to help you build a good test.

Since *what is being measured* affects test construction and interpretation, Section 1 points out guides for assessing achievement in specific subjects. The section is divided into ten subject areas: the arts, career and vocational education, English/language arts, foreign languages, home economics, mathematics, physical education, reading, science, and social studies. Each reference listed contains sample items, instruments, or frameworks for assessment that can be freely adapted. A few of the publications list sources of *unpublished* instruments. Many contain advice on what to do and what not to do when measuring in the subject field. The validity of the instruments put at your disposal through these books may or may not be well established.

Section 2 lists articles and books that explain how to construct written tests, regardless of subject and how to convert raw scores to norm scores, should the need arise.

Section 3 describes three sources of uncopyrighted test items. These sources are non-profit and public organizations which have compiled educational objectives and test items. The items may be reproduced without legal restriction.

A list of publishers who offer to "do it all" for you comprises Section 4. These test services will put together a test to your specifications, to fit your program. The listing implies no endorsement of these relatively new services. Since a good evaluation of their quality remains to be done, if you choose this alternative, you are venturing into uncharted waters.

Finally, Section 5 lists articles and books for further reading. These should enable you to find out more about major concepts and issues in achievement testing, and particularly about the relevance of criterion-referenced and norm-referenced approaches to test construction and score interpretation.

As a check on the quality of the items in the test you do eventually produce, consult Appendix B, page 53, A Reminder of Some Common Item Construction Errors.

Section 1: Subject-Oriented Publications on How To
Assess Achievement

The Arts

Stake, R. E., et al. *Evaluating the arts in education: A responsive approach.* Columbus, Ohio: Charles E. Merrill Publishing, 1975.

Chapters by several authors in this book explore the problem of just what an evaluator should consider in assessing the arts in schools. "Arts" is intended to encompass graphic arts, theatre, dance, music, film, and television. The chapters by Stake and McLean should be particularly helpful in terms of suggesting an overall approach to evaluating arts education.

The responsive evaluation advocated by Stake devotes much time to observing the program in action, identifying issues that confront the program participants, addressing the questions that various evaluation audiences want answered, and interpreting the program as witnessed in light of the different value-perspectives inferred by the evaluator.

The chapter by L. D. McLean on "judging the quality of a school as a place where the arts might thrive" calls the evaluator's attention to the school environment as a whole, the suitability and accessibility of the work space allotted to arts activities, the artistic output of the school, and the support shown for artistic activities and output. McLean provides a series of charts that summarize the facts and judgments which such an evaluation should take into account.

The book ends with a bibliography that includes abstracts of 28 readings in evaluation and arts education, annotated references for 10 evaluation reports, 62 references for topics of interest, and descriptive references for 9 other sourcebooks that could be helpful to an evaluator of arts education.

Thomas, R. M. Rationale for measurement in the visual arts. *Educational and Psychological Measurement,* 1965, *25*(1), 163-189.

After reviewing the chief faults of most art tests, the author proposes four features that should characterize future attempts at measurement in art:

1. Provision for measuring a greater variety of factors that compose products and art abilities.
2. More adequate distinctions among the abilities involved in appreciation, criticism, and production of art.
3. Test norms that are adaptable to different schools or philosophies of art.
4. A more adequate treatment of the creativity dimension.

The author then attempts to outline strategies for constructing tests that accomplish the first three of these goals, while admitting that his proposal "does relatively little to solve the problem of measuring creativity."

The author discusses separately measures of art preference, art analysis, and art production, which he says are needed to measure both aptitude and achievement. In each of these three cateogries, he provides illustrative items, describes the range of content coverage that he thinks is desirable, and discusses considerations of test format and administration.

Evaluators of programs in the visual arts will appreciate this article either for its advice concerning test construction or for its provision of models and standards against which to assess published instruments.

Career and Vocational Education

Hardaway, M. *Testing and evaluation in business education.* Cincinnati, Ohio: Southwestern Publishing, 1966.

After discussing general considerations involved in the development of a testing program and the construction of tests, the author provides many types of sample test items for measuring business, bookkeeping and accounting, clerical and secretarial knowledge and skills, as well as a few items dealing with personnel communication, office management, and other topics relevant to business education.

Warmbrod, J. R. *Criterion-referenced instruments for assessment of specialized vocational agriculture programs: Final report.* Columbus Ohio:

Ohio State University, Dept. of Agricultural Education, 1974. (Abstract in *Resources in Education,* 1976, *11*(3). ED 113 547.)

According to the ERIC abstract, "criterion referenced, field-tested instruments developed to assess 11th and 12th grade vocational agriculture education programs in (1) agricultural mechanics, (2) horticulture, (3) agribusiness supplies and services, and (4) farm management are presented in the document. A narrative report briefly discusses objectives; test construction; field testing, which involved administering the test to 12th grade students in 16 area vocational centers and 10 local schools; and the program's contribution to education. Appended materials make up the body of the document ... and consist of: an extensive treatment of test objectives and the mastery tests for each of the four areas, a list of schools in which field testing was done, and 24 tables giving item analysis and summary statistics for each test. . . ."

English and Language Arts

Cooper, C. R. Holistic evaluation of writing. In C. R. Cooper & L. Odell, *Evaluating writing: Describing, measuring, judging.* Urbana, Illinois: National Council of Teachers of English, 1977.

This chapter provides a number of rating scales and dichotomous (yes/no) scales for making a series of overall judgments about a piece of student writing. The scales included were designed for three types of writing: expository (explanatory) writing, personal narrative writing, and dramatic writing. The author argues for the validity of these procedures, and discusses methods for improving the reliability of rater judgments.

Diederich, P. B. *Measuring growth in English.* Urbana, Illinois: National Council of Teachers of English, 1974.

The author's major purpose is to provide procedures for making essay grading more reliable. The book includes descriptive criteria that can be used by raters to determine the level of adequacy of a piece of writing with respect to eight factors. The author also discusses how to establish acceptable topics for test essays and maintain secrecy in the final determination of the stimulus content of the essay test. The book ends with 96 statements of qualities that are usually desirable in writing, some of which may be useful as objectives in teaching writing skills.

Fagan, W. T., Cooper, C. R., & Jensen, J. M. *Measures for research and evaluation in the English language arts.* Urbana, Illinois: ERIC Clearinghouse on Reading and Communication Skills and National Council of Teachers of English, 1975.

This book systematically describes 87 instruments that test various aspects of English language arts education. Among these instruments are 23 tests of reading skills, 15 tests of achievement in literature, 14 tests of language development, 14 tests of writing skills, and 9 tests of standard English as a second language or dialect. Information is provided about each instrument's purpose; when it was constructed; the appearance, organization, and administration of the items; the nature and extent of validity, reliability, and normative data available; and how to order the instrument. Also, in the majority of cases, the book includes sample items from the tests.

In order to be selected for inclusion in the book, each of the 87 instruments was first judged

- "suitable for assessing a component of the field of English education,"
- "readily available to the potential user," and
- "*not* available commercially."

The authors' intention was to make accessible to language arts teachers a variety of potential achievement measures.

Foreign Languages

Valette, R. M. *Modern language testing*. New York: Harcourt Brace Jovanovich, 1977.

Although this book contains some general advice concerning measurement of achievement in foreign language education, it is primarily a resource of *item types* suitable for testing various aspects of foreign language learning. The important features of each item type are described, and a sample is then provided in most cases.

Item types are provided for listening comprehension, speaking, reading comprehension, writing competence, comprehension of the culture, and knowledge of literature. In addition, several scales are provided for rating proficiency in speaking a foreign language. The final chapter provides seven item types for constructing an informal oral test of bilingual competence in listening and speaking.

In an appendix on commercially available language tests, the author describes various tests of foreign languages under the headings, "achievement tests" and "proficiency tests." The languages covered by these tests are French, Spanish, German, Russian, Italian, and Hebrew. A majority of these instruments test listening, reading, and writing skills; a minority also test speaking skills. Other tests described are general prognostic language aptitude tests, tests of English as a second language, a Spanish/English bilingual test for K-2, and a foreign language attitude questionnaire. All these commercially available tests are described rather than evaluated, and neither validity nor reliability information is provided.

Home Economics

Indiana Home Economics Association. *Evaluation in home economics.* West Lafayette, Indiana: University Book Store, 1974. (Abstract in *Resources in Education,* 1975, *10*(12). ED 109 334.)

The instruments included in this book are intended as resources for the evaluation of students and programs with respect to home economics education. The book begins with a discussion of tests, checklists, rating scales, and questionnaires. The authors recommend the use of a variety of measures in order to adequately assess different aspects of the program. The remainder of the book consists of sample instruments with suggestions for their use in evaluating knowledge and attitudes in the areas of child development, clothing and textiles, consumer education, foods and nutrition, housing and home decorating, and interpersonal relations.

While several of the sample instruments might be used in an evaluation study of a home economics program, most of the instruments appear to be more suitable as instructional aids than as evaluation tools. The tests do, however, sample a range of skills and possible instructional objectives; and they could serve as a basis for discussing which objectives are most crucial and which understandings and skills are most lacking in the students. After such an assessment of student needs, a critical review of the items in these instruments could help an evaluator in constructing a valid measure of the skills addressed by the program.

Mathematics

Suydam, M. N. *Unpublished instruments for evaluation in mathematics education: An annotated listing.* Columbus, Ohio: ERIC Information Analysis Center for Science, Mathematics and Environmental Education, 1974.

This list of tests is "intended as a reference [with] no endorsement . . . implied." References to 208 instruments relevant to math education are annotated. Each annotation contains a statement of what the instrument is designed to measure, the types of items, their format and number, the grade or age level with which the test has been used, and reliability and validity data.

Of the 208 annotated instruments, 172 are cognitive, 26 are affective, 7 are for analysis of teaching, and 3 are for research analysis. Of the cognitive tests, 7 are of algebra, 5 are of creativity, 7 are diagnostic, 7 are of preschool knowledge, 10 are of fractions, 41 are general, 16 are of geometry, 4 are of logic, 4 are of measurement, 4 are designed for mentally retarded students, 3 are of teaching methodology, 18 are of number systems, 7 are of operations (+, -, x, ÷), 12 are Piagetian-related, 6 are of problem-solving, 6 are reading-related, 2 are science-related, and 13 are miscellaneous. All annotated instruments are indexed by type and by author.

Many instruments are cited on a supplementary list; but these are referenced only, not described in detail.

Physical Education

American Alliance for Health, Physical Education and Recreation. *Testing for impaired, disabled, and handicapped individuals.* Washington: Author, 1976.

This booklet gives descriptive and evaluative information about tests in three categories:

- Physical fitness tests (13 tests reviewed). Preceding the descriptions of each test, a comparative overview of their content is provided.
- Motor ability, perceptual motor development, and psychomotor tests (27 tests reviewed). A chart comparing coverage of these tests with respect to 13 component skills (including visual, auditory, tactile, and coordination skills) precedes the separate descriptions of the tests.
- Developmental profiles (9 tests reviewed). Their content is compared and analyzed in terms of the following aspects of development: adaptive behavior, basic knowledge, communication, fine and gross motor skills, personal/social and practical skills, reasoning, self-care, and visual perception.

Each test description lists what is measured and tells how it is measured and how the test is administered and scored.

Finally, 10 locally developed assessment devices are presented at the end of the booklet "to show a variety of locally developed devices and approaches used for both formal testing and informal assessment purposes."

Hunsicker, P., & Reiff, G. G. *Youth fitness test manual.* Washington: American Alliance for Health, Physical Education, and Recreation, 1975.

This booklet presents six tests of physical fitness with accompanying percentile norms based on national samples for ages 10 through 17. Separate norms for males and females are provided. The first test is really two different tests—"pull up: boys" and "flexed-arm hang: girls." The other tests—sit up, shuttle run, standing broad jump, 50 yard dash, and 600-yard run-walk—are the same for both sexes. Complete directions for administering all tests are provided.

Percentiles for each age are supplemented by percentiles based on a classification index that takes age, height, and weight into account.

Johnson, B. L., & Nelson, J. K. *Practical measurements for evaluation in physical education.* Minneapolis, Minnesota: Burgess, 1974.

This book describes a host of tests in the field of physical education, in many cases providing norms and complete instructions for carrying out the tests. Where this is not done, bibliographic references are supplied. Some of the tests only have norms for college men and women, but others include norms for a broad range of ages.

In addition to describing and referencing a variety of physical fitness and motor ability test batteries, measures of particular physical factors are included in the book. The authors describe 8 tests of flexibility, 10 of strength, 9 of muscular endurance, 6 of cardiovascular condition, 6 of power, 7 of agility, 8 of balance, 7 dealing with reaction and/or speed, 6 of rhythm and dance, 8 rating scales and 9 objective instruments for measuring posture, 4 tests of kinesthetic perception, and 3 perceptual-motor test batteries.

In a long chapter on sports skills, tests for skills in the sports of archery, badminton, basketball, football, golf, gymnastics for women, soccer, softball and baseball, tennis, and volleyball are presented—with norms; and tests for skills in bowling, handball, speedball, and swimming are described with references to sources of more information.

The book provides descriptions, sample items, and references for six measures dealing with leadership, social behavior, and acceptance of status within a group. In addition, one measure of attitude toward physical education is presented in its entirety, and seven other attitude scales dealing with sports and physical activity are described, along with sample items and sources for obtaining entire instruments.

Finally, the authors include a bibliography of journals and theses containing tests of knowledge of particular sports and of topics in physical education.

Reading

Miller, W. H. *Reading diagnostic kit.* New York: The Center for Applied Research in Education, 1974.

Potter, T. C., & Rae, G. *Informal reading diagnosis: A practical guide for the classroom teacher.* Englewood Cliffs, New Jersey: Prentice-Hall, 1973.

These two books are similar in content. They can both serve as a source of informal reading tests that can be freely reproduced or adapted to local needs. There are instruments in both books that measure oral and silent reading skills, word recognition or decoding skills, and attitudes and interests related to reading.

The book by Miller includes a number of reading-observation check-lists and projective-technique instruments to help determine causes of reading difficulties. Miller also provides descriptive evaluations of six standardized reading tests and two listening-comprehension tests.

The book by Potter and Rae contains other kinds of instruments related to reading, such as tests measuring auditory, visual, and tactile discrimination; memory; listening and repeating; generative language skills; following directions; listening comprehension; study skills; and literary interpretation.

Science

Berey, D. *Earth science.* (High School Exams and Answer Series, Grades 9-12.) Woodbury, New York: Barron's Educational Series, 1976.

Edwards, G., & Blifeld, M. *Biology.* (High School Exams and Answer Series.) Woodbury, New York: Barron's Educational Series, 1977.

Gerwitz, H. *Physics.* (Regents Exams and Answer Series, Grades 10-12). Woodbury, New York: Barron's Educational Series, 1976.

Test item book for biological science: Inquiry into life. Boulder, Colorado: Biological Sciences Curriculum Study, 1968.

Test item book for biological science: Molecules to man. Boulder, Colorado: Biological Sciences Curriculum Study, 1973.

Test item book for biological science: An ecological approach. Boulder, Colorado: Biological Sciences Curriculum Study, 1973.

Walsh, M. J. *Chemistry.* (High School Exams and Answer Series, Grades 9-12.) Woodbury, New York: Barron's Educational Series, 1977.

The titles listed above are all sources of test items for measuring basic cognitive learning in science courses at the secondary school level. Program evaluators may want to use these tests as a basis for generating new test items that more closely match the program being studied.

Mayer, V. J. *Unpublished evaluation instruments in science education: A handbook.* Columbus, Ohio: ERIC/SMEAC Reference Center, Ohio State University, College of Education, 1974.

Each of the science education instruments described in this guide employs an objective scoring system. None of them is commercially published. Most of the instruments referenced are available from the ERIC Document Service, or a journal, author, or sponsoring institution.

Those which are not are included in their entirety in the appendix of the instruments handbook itself.

Every instrument description tells what the instrument measures; the number and types of items and subtests; the educational level (and, in some cases, the geographic area) of the students with whom the test has been used; the reliability data reported and the size of the group used for determining reliability; means and standard deviations of groups tested, where available; procedures used for validating the instrument, if any; and how to acquire a copy of the instrument.

The instruments are organized into six groups. The first group deals with knowledge and understanding of ideas, facts, and principles. The first chapter describes 21 tests of this kind in biology, 22 in earth science, 49 in physics and chemistry, and 26 in general science.

The second group of tests deals with "the ability to effectively engage in the processes and skills involved in scientific inquiry." Thirty-two tests of this type are described.

The third group of instruments deals with student characteristics relevant to science education, such as cognitive preferences, critical thinking, and creative thinking. Sixteen instruments of this kind are reviewed.

The fourth group of instruments attempts to measure student attitudes and interests related to science. Twenty-six instruments focus on science or scientists; 22 focus on taking science classes or being a science teacher; and 10 focus on conservation, drug abuse, environment, radioactivity, and sex.

The fifth group of tests measures knowledge of the nature and limits of scientific pursuits and of their interrelationship with other social and economic processes. Fifteen measures of this type are described.

The sixth group of instruments deals with the pedagogy of science education. Twenty-one instruments focus on perceptions of science classroom practices, 10 on attitudes toward classroom practices and curricula, 6 on teacher supervision and evaluation, 5 on course content, 1 on teacher expectations of students, and 1 on facilities for science education.

Social Studies

National Council for the Social Studies. *Thirty-fifth yearbook: Evaluation in social studies.* Washington: Author, 1965.

There are many chapters in this yearbook that suggest useful measurement techniques and illustrate principles with sample test items. The following chapters appear to be particularly helpful:

- The objective test item, Berg, H. D., 47-76

- Evaluation of critical thinking in the social studies, Chausow, H. M., 77-99
- Improving the essay test in the social studies, Solomon, R. J., 137-153
- Planning, assembling, and administering the objective test, 174-201

Since this book was published in 1965, the bibliography of published tests is somewhat dated. However, if used in conjunction with some of the more recent editions of the reference tools cited in Chapter 2, such as Hoepfner or Buros, the descriptive survey provided by this bibliography can still be useful.

Senathirajah, N., & Weiss, J. *Evaluation in geography: A resource book for teachers.* Toronto: Ontario Institute for Studies in Education, 1971.

Three chapters give practical assistance to the evaluator who wants to construct a written test in geography. Examples of a variety of cognitive objectives in geography are included, showing how test items of both the multiple-choice variety and the fill-in type can measure the attainment of complex understandings as well as simple knowledge. The authors also provide suggestions for more reliable scoring of short essay responses to questions in geography. The book includes brief discussions of categorization schemes for objectives and plans for developing a test-item pool from which to sample in putting together a well-balanced test.

Social education. *Journal of the National Council for the Social Studies,* Nov.-Dec., 1976, *40,* 503-541 and 567-582.

This issue has two sections that deal with measuring achievement in social studies. The first section, "Testing in the social studies," is intended "to provide ideas and information about social studies test development that teachers might find useful in their classroom situations." The topics included are: rationales for testing; standardized tests; and teacher-made tests in world history, American history, political science, economics, and multiethnic studies. Illustrative sample items are included in the articles on teacher-made tests.

The second relevant section, "Social studies and the elementary teacher: Informal assessment of social studies learning," tries to provide "a rationale . . . and examples of techniques and procedures" for evaluation of elementary school students' learning in social studies. The examples were developed and used by teachers. Four evaluation strategies are outlined, and different ways of obtaining and recording meaningful data are illustrated.

Superka, D. P., Vigliani, A., & Hedstrom, J. E. *Social studies evaluation sourcebook.* (A forthcoming publication, No. 227, from the Social Science Education Consortium, 855 Broadway, Boulder, CO 80302.)

This sourcebook should be of assistance in deciding what instruments or strategies to use in measuring achievement in the social studies. For more information, contact the Consortium.

Section 2: Readings in How To Construct and Norm an Achievement Test

How-To Guides to Testing in General

Educational Testing Service. *Making the classroom test: A guide for teachers.* Princeton, New Jersey: Author, 1973. (Abstract in *Research in Education,* 1974, *9*(1), ED 081 784.)

Gerberich, J. R., Green, H. A., & Jorgensen, A. N. Constructing and using classroom tests and techniques: Measuring and evaluating in the school subjects. In *Measurement and evaluation in the modern school.* New York: David McKay Company, 1962, 199-295, 347-567.

Gronlund, N. E. *Constructing achievement tests.* Englewood Cliffs, New Jersey: Prentice-Hall, 1977.

Gronlund, N. E. *Preparing criterion-referenced tests for classroom instruction.* New York: The Macmillan Company, 1973.

Kryspin, W. J., & Feldhusen, J. F. *Developing classroom tests: A guide for writing and evaluating test items.* Minneapolis, Minnesota: Burgess, 1974.

Payne, D. A. Constructing short-answer achievement items; constructing and scoring essay items and tests. In *Assessment of learning: Cognitive and affective.* Lexington, Massachusetts: D. C. Heath and Company, 1974, 95-148.

Scannell, D. P., & Tracy, D. B. *Testing and measurement in the classroom.* Boston: Houghton Mifflin Company, 1975.

Sullivan, H. J., Baker, R. L., & Schutz, R. E. Developing instructional specifications. In R. L. Baker & R. E. Schutz (Eds.), *Instructional product development.* New York: Van Nostrand Reinhold, 1971.

Swezey, R. W., & Pearlstein, R. B. *Guidebook for developing criterion-referenced tests.* Arlington, Virginia: Army Research Institute for the Behavioral and Social Sciences, Report No. 287-AR 18(2)-IR-0974, August, 1975.

Wesman, A. G. Writing the test item. In R. L. Thorndike (Ed.), *Educational measurement.* Washington: American Council on Education, 1971, 81-129.

Writing and Revising Multiple-Choice and
True-False Items

Corbluth, J. Functional analysis of multiple-choice questions for reading comprehension. *English Language Teachers Journal,* 1975, *29,* 164-173.

Ebel, R. L. How to write multiple-choice test items. In *Essentials of educational measurement.* Englewood Cliffs, New Jersey: Prentice-Hall, 1972, 187-225.

Ebel, R. L. How to write true-false items. *Educational and Psychological Measurement,* 1971, *31,* 417-426.

Educational Testing Service. *Multiple choice questions: A close look.* Princeton, New Jersey: Author, 1973. (Abstract in *Research in Education,* 1974, *9*(1), ED 081 783.)

Wood, R. Multiple choice: A state of the art report. *Evaluation in Education: International Progress,* 1977, *1,* 191-280.

Derivation of Norm Scores With
Locally Constructed Instruments

Ebel, R. L. Percentile ranks; interpretation of percentile ranks; stanine standard scores. In *Essentials of educational measurement.* Englewood Cliffs, New Jersey: Prentice Hall, 1972, 285-296.

Gerberich, J. R., Green, H. A., & Jorgenson, A. N. Applying statistical procedures to measurement and evaluation results. In *Measurement and evaluation in the modern school.* New York: David McKay Company, 1962, 299-343.

Gronlund, N. E. Norm-referenced interpretation. In *Constructing achievement tests.* Englewood Cliffs, New Jersey: Prentice-Hall, 1977, 120-129.

Townsend, E. A., & Burke, P. J. *Using statistics in classroom instruction.* New York: Macmillan, 1975.

Section 3: Uncopyrighted Banks of Test Items
and Objectives

Behavioral objectives and test items. Downers Grove, Illinois: Institute for Educational Research.

    This is a source of about 5,000 objectives and 27,000 accompanying test items written by Chicago elementary and secondary school teachers as part of a workshop. These are available either from the Institute at

1400 W. Maple Avenue, Downers Grove, Illinois 60515, or from the ERIC Document Reproduction Service (ERIC numbers: ED 066 492 through 508). The series begins with a description of workshop procedures and is followed by attitude, math, language arts, social studies, and science items and objectives at four levels—primary, intermediate, junior high, and high school.

CO-OP objectives and items. Available from The CO-OP, 413 Hills House North, University of Massachusetts, Amherst, Massachusetts 01002.

This is a source of more than 10,000 objectives and 40,000 items for elementary and secondary school levels. They are presented in 47 booklets and were originally developed by a number of school systems and state education departments for their own use. The items test learnings in language arts, math, social studies, science, and vocational education. The booklets are described as varying in comprehensiveness and have not been edited by The CO-OP.

Individualized mathematical learning in the elementary schools—An ordered list of mathematical objectives, K-8; test items for primary mathematics; test items for intermediate mathematics.

These materials provide about 200 math objectives and 400 to 500 sample test items, keyed to the objectives. They were developed at the University of Wisconsin's R&D Center in cooperation with the Wisconsin Dept. of Public Instruction. Single copies may be purchased from CCL Document Service, 1025 W. Johnson St., Madison, Wisconsin 53706.

Section 4: Producers of Made-To-Order Tests

CTB/McGraw-Hill (ORBIT)
Del Monte Research Park
Monterey, California 93940

Houghton-Mifflin Company
(Customized Objective Monitoring Service)
777 California Avenue
Palo Alto, California 94304

Instructional Objectives Exchange
(IOX Test Development Service)
Box 24095
Los Angeles, California 90024

Multi-Media Associates, Inc.
(Customized Criterion-Referenced Tests)
P.O. Box 13052
Tucson, Arizona 85732

National Evaluation Systems, Inc.
(CAM—Comprehensive Achievement Monitoring)
P.O. Box 226
Amherst, Massachusetts 01002

Science Research Associates
(Mastery Custom Tests—Reading and Math)
155 North Wacker Drive
Chicago, Illinois 60606

Section 5: For Further Reading

Airasian, P. W., & Madaus, G. F. Criterion-referenced testing in the classroom. *Measurement and Education,* 1972, *3,* 73-88.

Anderson, R. C. How to construct achievement tests to assess comprehension. *Review of Educational Research,* 1972, *42,* 145-170.

Angoff, W. H. Criterion-referencing, norm-referencing, and the SAT. *College Board Review,* 1974, *92,* 3-5.

Angoff, W. H. Scales, norms, and equivalent scores. In R. L. Thorndike (Ed.), *Educational measurement.* Washington: American Council on Education, 1971, 508-600.

Baker, E. L. Beyond objectives: Domain-referenced tests for evaluation and instructional improvement. *Educational Technology,* 1974, *14*(6), 10-16.

Baker, E. L. Cooperation and the state of the world in criterion-referenced tests. *Educational Horizons,* 1974, *52*(4), 193-196.

Baker, E. L. *Using measurement to improve instruction.* (Abstract in *Research in Education,* 1973, *8*(3). ED 069 762.)

Beatty, W. H. (Ed.). *Improving educational assessment and an inventory of measures of affective behavior.* Washington: Association for Supervision and Curriculum Development, 1969.

Block, J. H. Criterion-referenced measurements: Potential. *School Review,* 1971, *79,* 289-298.

Block, J. H. (Ed.). *Mastery learning: Theory and practice.* New York: Holt, Rinehart and Winston, 1971.

Block, J. H. (Ed.). *Operating principles for mastery learning.* New York: Holt, Rinehart and Winston, 1971.

Boehm, A. E. Criterion-referenced assessment for the teacher. *Teachers College Record,* 1973, *75*(1), 117-126.

Bormuth, J. R. *On the theory of achievement test items.* Chicago: University of Chicago Press, 1970.

Brennan, R. L. Model for the use of achievement data in an instructional system. *Instructional Science,* 1975, *4*(2), 113-136.

Buros, O. K. Fifty years in testing: Some reminiscences, criticisms, and suggestions. *Educational Researcher,* 1977, *6*(7), 9-15.

Cartier, F. A. Criterion-referenced testing of language skills. *TESOL Quarterly,* 1968, *2*(1), 27-32. (Abstract in *Research in Education,* 1968, *3*(12), ED 020 515.)

Carver, R. P. Reading tests in 1970 versus 1980: Psychometric versus edumetric. *Reading Teacher,* 1972, *26*(3), 299-302.

Cornejo, R. J. Criterion-referenced assessment system for bilingual reading: SOBER-Espanol. *California Journal of Educational Research,* 1974, 25, 294-301.

Cox, R. C., & Vargas, J. S. Comparison of item selection techniques for norm-referenced and criterion-referenced tests. *Report No. BR-5-0253.* Pittsburgh, Pennsylvania: Learning Research and Development Center, University of Pittsburgh, 1966. (Abstract in *Research in Education,* 1967, *6,* ED 010 517.)

Crehan, K. D. Item analysis for teacher-made mastery tests. *Journal of Educational Measurement,* 1974, *11,* 255-262.

Crombag, H. F., & De Gruijter, D. N. (Eds.). *Contemporary issues in educational testing.* The Hague: Mouton and Company, 1974.

Cronbach, L. J. Comments on mastery learning and its implications for curriculum development. In E. W. Eisner (Ed.), *Confronting curriculum reform.* Boston: Little, Brown, 1971, 49-55.

Day, G. F. *Investigation into the use of criterion-referenced measurement in vocational and technical training.* (Abstract in *Resources in Education,* 1976, *11*(5), ED 115 933.)

Denham, C. H. *Score reporting and item selection in selected criterion-referenced and domain-referenced tests.* (Abstract in *Resources in Education,* 1977, *12*(8), ED 137 341.)

Dziuban, C. D., & Vickery, K. V. Criterion-referenced measurement: Some recent developments. *Educational Leadership,* 1973, *30*(5), 483-486.

Ebel, R. L. Case for true-false test items. *School Review,* 1970, *78,* 373-390.

Ebel, R. L. Content standard test scores. *Educational and Psychological Measurement.* 1962, *22*(1), 15-22.

Ebel, R. L. Criterion-referenced measurements: Limitations. *School Review,* 1971, *79,* 282-288.

Ebel, R. L. Criterion-referenced and norm-referenced measurements. In *Essentials of educational measurement.* Englewood Cliffs, New Jersey: Prentice-Hall, 1972, 83-86.

Esler, W. K., & Dziuban, C. D. Criterion referenced test: Some advantages and disadvantages for science instruction. *Science Education,* 1974, *58*(2), 171-174.

Farr, R. (Ed.). *Measurement and evaluation of reading.* New York: Harcourt, Brace and World, 1970.

Fremer, J. Criterion-referenced interpretations of survey achievement tests. *Test Development Memorandum 72-1.* Princeton, New Jersey: Educational Testing Service, 1972. (Abstract in *Research in Education,* 1972, *7*(11), ED 065 533.)

Gardner, E. F. Normative standard scores. *Educational and Psychological Measurement,* 1962, *22*(1), 7-14.

Glaser, R. Instructional technology and the measurement of learning outcomes: Some questions. *American Psychologist,* 1963, *18,* 519-521.

Glaser, R., & Nitko, A. J. Measurement in learning and instruction. In R. L. Thorndike (Ed.), *Educational measurement.* Washington: American Council on Education, 1971, 625-670.

Glaser, R., and Klaus, D. J. Proficiency measurement: Assessing human performance. In R. M. Gagne (Ed.), *Psychological principles in system development.* New York: Holt, Rinehart and Winston, 1962, 419-474.

Good, T. L., Biddle, B. J., & Brophy, J. E. Criterion-referenced testing. In *Teachers make a difference.* New York: Holt, Rinehart and Winston, 1975.

Haladyna, T. M. Effects of different samples on item and test characteristics of criterion-referenced tests. *Journal of Education,* 1974, *11,* 93-99.

Hambleton, R. K. Testing and decision-making procedures for selected individualized instructional programs. *Review of Educational Research,* 1974, *44,* 371-400.

Hambleton, R. K., & Gorth, W. P. Criterion-referenced testing: Issues and applications. (Abstract in *Research in Education,* 1972, *7*(6), ED 060 025.)

Handy, J., & Johnstone, A. H. How students reason in objective tests. *Education in Chemistry,* 1973, *10,* 90-100.

Harris, C. W., Alkin, M. C., & Popham, W. J. (Eds.). Problems in criterion-referenced measurement. *CSE Monograph Series in Evaluation No. 3.* Los Angeles: Center for the Study of Evaluation, UCLA Graduate School of Education, 1974.

Harris, C. W., Pearlman, A., & Wilcox, R. Achievement test items: Methods of study. *CSE Monograph Series in Evaluation No. 6.* Los Angeles: Center for the Study of Evaluation, UCLA Graduate School of Education, 1977.

Hively, W. (Ed.). *Domain referenced testing.* Englewood Cliffs, New Jersey: Educational Technology Publications, 1974.

Hively, W., Patterson, H. L., & Page, S. H. "Universe-defined" system of arithmetic achievement tests. *Journal of Educational Measurement,* 1968, *5*(4), 275-290.

Jackson, R. *Developing criterion-referenced tests.* Princeton, New Jersey: Educational Testing Service, ERIC Clearinghouse on Tests, Measurement, and Evaluation, 1970. (Abstract in *Research in Education,* 1970, *5*(11), ED 041 052.)

King, F. J. *Content referenced interpretive system for standardized reading tests: Final report.* Urbana, Illinois: National Council of Teachers of English, 1974. (Abstract in *Resources in Education,* 1976, *11*(1), ED 110 978.)

Klein, S. P., & Kosecoff, J. Issues and procedures in the development of criterion referenced tests. *TM Report 26,* 1973, 1-18. (Abstract in *Research in Education,* 1974, *9*(2), ED 083 284.)

McClelland, D. C. Testing for competence rather than for "intelligence." *American Psychologist,* 1973, *28,* 1-14.

Martuza, V. R. *Applying norm-referenced and criterion-referenced measurement in education.* Boston: Allyn and Bacon, 1977.

Mehrens, W. A., & Lehmann, I. J. Norm- and criterion-referenced measurement. In *Measurement and evaluation in education and psychology.* New York: Holt, Rinehart and Winston, 1973, 63-76.

Metfessel, N. S., & Michael, W. B. Paradigm involving multiple criterion measures for the evaluation of the effectiveness of school programs. *Educational and Psychological Measurement,* 1967, *27* 931-943.

Millman, J. Criterion-referenced measurement. In W. J. Popham (Ed.), *Evaluation in education: Current applications.* Berkeley, California: McCutchan, 1974.

Millman, J. Program assessment, criterion-referenced tests, and things like that. *Educational Horizons,* 1974, *52*(4), 188-192.

Oakland, T. *Evaluation of available models for estimating the reliability and validity of criterion-referenced measures.* (Abstract in *Research in Education,* 1972, *7*(11), ED 065 589.)

Osburn, H. G. Item sampling for achievement testing. *Educational and Psychological Measurement,* 1968, *28,* 95-104.

Popham, W. J. *Criterion-referenced measurement.* Englewood Cliffs, New Jersey: Prentice-Hall, 1978.

Popham, W. J. (Ed.). *Criterion-referenced measurement: An introduction.* Englewood Cliffs, New Jersey: Educational Technology Publications, 1971.

Popham, W. J., & Husek, T. R. Implications of criterion-referenced measurement. *Journal of Educational Measurement,* 1969, *6*(1), 1-9.

Popham, W. J. Instructional objectives exchange: New support for criterion-referenced instruction. *Phi Delta Kappan,* 1970, *52*(3), 174-175.

Prescott, G. A. Criterion-referenced test interpretation in reading. *Reading Teacher,* 1971, *24,* 347-354.

Roudabush, G. E. Item selection for criterion-referenced tests. (Abstract in *Research in Education,* 1973, *8*(7), ED 074 147.)

Sanders, J. R., & Murray, S. L. Alternatives for achievement testing. *Educational Technology,* 1976, *16*(3), 17-23.

Shoemaker, D. M. Toward a framework for achievement testing. *Review of Educational Research,* 1975, *45*(1), 127-147.

Simon, G. B. Comments on "Implications of criterion-referenced measurement." *Journal of Educational Measurement,* 1969, *6*(4), 259-260.

Skager, R. W. Great criterion-referenced test myth. *CSE Report No. 95.* Los Angeles: Center for the Study of Evaluation, UCLA Graduate School of Education, 1978.

Upshur, J. A. Language proficiency testing and the contrastive analysis dilemma. *Language Learning,* 1962, *12,* 123-127.

Ward, J. On the concept of criterion-referenced measurement. *British Journal of Educational Psychology*, 1970, *40*, 314-323.

Young, J. C., Knapp, R. R., & Michael, W. B. Validity of the *Tests of Achievement in Basic Skills* for predicting achievement in general mathematics and algebra. *Educational and Psychological Measurement*, 1970, *30*, 951-954.

Chapter 5

Validity and Reliability of Achievement Measures

The purpose of this chapter is to present you with an informal introduction to the subjects of reliability and validity. You might use the information here either as a guide for determining the quality of the instruments you construct yourself or as a set of general principles to bear in mind when reading and interpreting the manuals that accompany the tests you purchase. To give you a concrete situation on which to pin the new information presented here, try to read with a particular achievement test in mind, imagining how the discussion applies to *it*.

If the instrument whose reliability and validity you will be examining is a *criterion-referenced* test for which you will interpret scores *per objective*, then each segment of the instrument that addresses one particular objective must be considered a distinct test. Questions about validity and reliability will need to be asked about each separately.

Assessments of validity and reliability help to determine the amount of faith people should place in a measurement instrument. *Validity* and *reliability* refer to different aspects of a measure's *believability*. Judgments of *validity* answer the question: Is the instrument an appropriate one for what needs to be measured? *Reliability* indicators answer the question: Does the instrument yield consistent results? For obvious reasons, these are questions you must ask about any measure you select whether you buy it or construct it yourself. It may be helpful to remember that *valid* has the same root as *valor* and *value*, referring to strength or worth. Validity indicates how worthwhile a measure is likely to be, in a given situation, for telling you what you need to know. Validity boils down to whether the instrument is giving you the true story, or at least something approximating the truth.

Reliability, when used to refer to tests, carries the same meaning as when it refers to friends. A reliable friend is one on whom you can count to behave the same way time and again. Tests that give you essentially the same results when re-administered are reliable in this sense.

Please note that reliability refers to consistency, but consistency does not guarantee *truthfulness*. A friend, for instance, who compliments your taste in clothes each time he sees you is certainly reliable but may not necessarily be telling the truth. What is more, he may not even be deliberately misleading you. It may be just a habit, or perhaps his judgment is skewed by an appreciation of your many other good features. It could be that both you and your friend have terrible taste when viewed from some broader perspective! Similarly, an instrument's being reliable does *not* mean that it is a good measure of what it seems to measure.

Consider an example from one of the pioneer individualized Early Childhood programs of the 60's. Students demonstrated their progress by passing five-item criterion-referenced "Curriculum Accompanied Tests" (CATs) administered at the end of each unit in, for example, mathematics. Most of the CAT's had a fill-in-the-blanks format and were scored by classroom aides. First graders completing a unit on addition of one-digit numerals could *not* go on to tackle two-digit addition until they had passed the appropriate CAT. Student progress with this procedure seemed rapid. Some second graders were working at long-division and fractions! Skeptical about their own apparent success, program developers gave spot quizzes in math. They found that some of the second graders working on advanced units had trouble with simple addition. Puzzled, the developers administered the addition and multiplication CATs over and over. Sure enough, the children passed them. The tests were reliable. The problem was that the children had figured out a strategy for filling in blanks on the test forms without computing. The hastily developed CATs were filled with *response bias*. The lesson the curriculum developers learned was that reliable tests usually measure *something*, but not necessarily what you might think they measure.

Is a valid measure reliable? In general, yes. A valid test is one that has demonstrated its power to detect some *real* ability, attitude, or prevailing situation that the test user can identify and characterize. If the ability or skill being measured is itself stable, and if respondents' answers to the items are not affected by other unpredictable factors, then each administration of the instrument should yield essentially the same results.

A demonstration of reliability, therefore, is necessary but not conclusive evidence that an instrument is valid. All the reliability studies in the world will not guarantee validity—though they will help support a strong case for it. Bear this in mind particularly when reading about the technical adequacy of published tests. Since reliability is easier to demonstrate than validity, the technical manuals that accompany tests often report reliability data only. The publisher intends to imply validity through a demonstration of reliability. This is poor practice and amounts to doing half the job. Administrators need more adequate information if they are to justify using the test for making important decisions.

Validity: Is the Instrument an Appropriate One To Measure What You Want To Know?

Time and effort are invested in measurement for one of two reasons:

1. There is a need to detect *how much* of something—a skill, attitude, or ability a person has. This is a descriptive function of measurement. Both normed and criterion-referenced achievement tests are commonly used to assess how much knowledge or skill a student has acquired, though the *standards* used to decide successful performance differ.

2. There is a need to predict some *other,* possibly future, performance or state of the person, usually for the purpose of making a decision about her. When a test serves a predictive function, the primary interest is in obtaining a sample of present behavior upon which to base an expectation about how a person will perform in another, more complex setting. This is the case with test use for making decisions about placement in special programs.

When you use a test, you want to know you can rely on it to accomplish one of these two things. In either case, the instrument must provide a *sample of behavior* that supports conclusions about performance in a broader, more real-life context. The validity of a test reflects the sureness with which you can draw such conclusions. In fact, it will serve you well to think of validity as *the extent to which you can rule out interpretations of an instrument's results other than the one you wish to make.* Establishing a test's validity requires that you anticipate the potential arguments skeptics might use to dismiss its results. The credibility of your evaluation will be profoundly affected by the perceived validity of your measures. For this reason, you should include an assessment, even if informal, of each test's validity in your evaluation report. *Four major* approaches to determining if an instrument is valid have evolved during the history of testing. Each represents a different aspect of the problem of building a case for the appropriateness of the test for given situations. Three of the approaches have derived from using tests for description— determining how much of a skill people possess. The fourth approach focuses on the usefulness of the test as a predictor of future behavior.

Approach 1. Descriptive Use of an Instrument: Construct Validity

The word *construct* is a handy one for discussing measurement instruments. It is a catch-all term used to refer to the skill, attitude, or ability that an instrument is intended to measure. "Ability to add decimals," "attitude toward school," "need for achievement," "spatial ability," are all constructs. *The construct validity of a test is the extent to which you can be sure it represents the construct whose name appears in its title.* In a criterion-referenced test, construct validity means how well the test matches the objective it is supposed to measure. A test with good construct validity can be considered a substitute for actually observing a person displaying the skill in everyday life. To adequately defend the construct validity of the test, other explanations for what the test measures must be satisfactorily ruled out.

The ease of demonstrating construct validity for a particular instrument depends largely on the specificity of the construct itself. Sometimes the construct to be measured is one for which representative test items can be written with reasonable ease. This is the case with the ability to multiply fractions, answer questions about bonds in organic chemistry, or take shorthand dictation. In these situations, most people can agree about what a demonstration of the construct's existence would look like. Therefore, defending the instrument's validity simply requires describing how the instrument was developed and administered and comparing it with similar published instruments, if such exist.

Often, though, the construct to be measured is fuzzy, imprecise, or complex. This is particularly the case when a test is needed to measure *higher order* skills such as problem solving, essay writing, creativity, and other representations of complex human achievement. No clear, widely accepted definitions yet exist for these. In such cases, demonstrating construct validity demands a preliminary step—precise construct definition.

Construct definition. Before the validity of a test can be determined—actually before the test is developed—the construct which it measures must be defined as precisely as possible.[16] Defining the construct means explaining what is meant by, say, "good narrative style," "creative problem solving," or "the student will write an original sonnet" and pointing out how this definition might differ from those given by others. The definition should encompass the following:

1. If the construct in question is a complex one, then it should be depicted by means of a *list* or *graph,* as in Figure 5, page 97, *showing what a person with more—or perhaps less—of the construct might do.* The graph shows the construct's subcomponents composed of simpler and more discrete behaviors. A person with a *single* general test for

---

16. Writers on the topic of criterion-referenced tests usually talk about constructs in terms of one or more behavior domains, emphasizing that these tests sample from and predict observable performances. For a highly readable discussion of *domain definition,* as well as issues surrounding the reliability and validity of these measures, see Popham, W. J. *Criterion-referenced measurement.* Englewood Cliffs, NJ: Prentice-Hall, 1978.

assessing the whole construct would have to make sure she covered all its subcomponents within one instrument. The developer of criterion-referenced tests could either write a single general test to cover the construct *or* try to write a short separate test to measure one or two subcomponents at a time. In this case a whole *battery* of tests would address the construct.

2. A description should be prepared of closely related constructs with which the construct in question might be confused. It should include an argument about why this construct is distinct from those and worthy of separate measurement.

When this construct description underpins a general test of a high-level ability, it helps the test developer justify that the skill she is attempting to measure is a real factor influencing behavior. It does this by requiring that she anticipate and answer arguments to the contrary. She must show, for example, that the behaviors she claims describe "creative problem solving" are not actually better ascribed to "general intelligence" or "divergent thinking." She will also need to answer the challenge that "creative problem solving" is too multifaceted to be measured, since it manifests itself differently in different people.

Once construct definition has been satisfactorily accomplished, the developer still must show that the *test itself* is valid. This means that the test measures the degree of presence of the construct that she has defined. Usually, showing construct validity of an instrument amounts to demonstrating that it overcomes extraneous sources of bias, such as ability to "psych out the test" and give only desirable answers, and that its scores are closely related to scores on other measures of the construct.

Be careful that the test you choose for your evaluation is construct valid for your particular purpose. In other words, make sure the construct underlying the test is the one you want to measure. If, for instance, you want to know how adequately a vocational education program has prepared students to read and write on the job, then the test must address itself to *the real world construct,* not merely to the content of the course of instruction given via the program. This is another way of saying that a test based only on the program, with items presented in the formats used for instruction, *can be considered valid only for measuring within-program achievement.* While within-program achievement might well be related to overall performance in the skill area in question, you cannot claim that a program-specific test demonstrates this. When designing an achievement test for program evaluation you must decide, then, on the precise nature of the construct to be measured: Do you wish to show that the program has developed student ability to perform in the world beyond the program, or will you and your audience be satisfied with demonstrating that students have at least achieved what was taught to them? If you have an interest in demonstrating both, of course, this can be done. Address part of your measure to each of the two concerns, or construct separate tests.

Defending construct validity. Armed with a detailed description of the construct to be measured, the test developer can support the validity of a test in several ways:

1. *Opinions of judges.* Suppose you were preparing a test to determine whether students can write letters of application for jobs. The test might consist of a set of newspaper ads describing fictitious jobs for which students must reply. You can get an idea of the validity of this test by showing it to a group of judges—perhaps curriculum specialists, or teachers, or employers themselves. Ask the judges to make a list of particular skills related to writing application letters that, in their opinion, will be picked up by the instrument. The test can be considered construct valid to the extent that their lists fit your construct definition. What is more, if the judges' individual conclusions about what the instrument seems to be measuring agree with each other as well, then you have even stronger evidence of construct validity.

   Using the opinions of judges to assess an instrument's validity, you should be warned, will produce credible results to the extent that the judges merit the trust of your audience. If the judges themselves lack qualifications, or if they stand to benefit from instrument bias, then their judgments will be vulnerable to challenge.

2. *Correlations.* [17] Another way of establishing construct validity is to administer a second, different test of the same or a *related* construct to the same group of people. Then the results of the two measures can be correlated. You might, for instance, be able to show that your measure of "effective writing" correlates positively with indicators of other language arts skills such as grammatical usage, effective speech, or high reading aptitude. You might also show that your measure of effective writing has a *negative* correlation with detectors of language arts pro-

---

17. Correlations are mentioned often throughout this chapter. Correlation refers to the strength of the relationship between two measures. A high *positive* correlation means that people scoring high on one measure also score high on the other. A *negative* correlation also shows a strong relationship but in the opposite direction. *No* correlation means that knowing a person's score on one measure does not educate your guess about his score on the other. Correlations are usually expressed by a *correlation coefficient,* a decimal between −1 and +1, calculated from peoples' scores on the two different measures. Since there are several different correlation coefficients, each depending on the type of instruments being used, discussion of how to perform correlations to determine validity or reliability is outside the scope of this book. The various correlation coefficients are discussed in most statistics texts, however. You might also refer to Fitz-Gibbon, C. T., & Morris, L. L. How to calculate statistics. In L. L. Morris (Ed.), *Program evaluation kit.* Beverly Hills: Sage Publications, 1978.

blems such as diagnostic measures of speech disfunction. A whole methodology using "Multi-Trait, Multi-Method Matrices"[18] has evolved for estimating validity by means of a table of correlations with measures similar to and different from the one in question.

Correlational methods for supporting test validity are not often used with criterion-referenced tests because the scores from these tests may not have sufficient variability to produce a useful correlation coefficient.[19]

3. *Criterion group studies.* If possible, the test could be administered to a group of people already judged to possess an abundance or deficiency of the construct in question. Demonstrating, for instance, that people reputed to be good writers score well on a "creative writing" test and that people judged low, score low builds a strong case for the instrument's validity. Criterion group studies are wise to perform, particularly if you are developing an instrument yourself. In addition to assessing validity, they help you to identify items that are inadequate for measuring the construct or which give unreliable responses. Discarding these items will improve the quality of the instrument, increasing both its validity and reliability.

4. *Appeal to logic.* Many times, particularly when the construct can be easily defined, audiences will accept the instrument as logically related to the construct, as long as they know that it has been *administered fairly,* that is:

- Enough time has been allowed for its administration so that the respondents are not rushed.
- Hints and clues about the proper way to answer are absent from the instrument's format or instructions.
- There is no bias in the scoring.

In every instance where you use a test, you are asking not only that the audience accept the instrument's representation of the construct, but also that they accept the *circumstances of its administration,* and do not view these circumstances as having invalidated the results.

Demonstrating a test's construct validity, it should be apparent, is not an all-or-nothing matter. The demonstration can rely on any combination of the types of evidence described here. If you plan to use an instrument

18. See Campbell, D. A., & Fiske, D. W. Validation by the multitrait multi-method matrix. *Psychological Bulletin,* 1959, *56,* 81-105.

19. An exception to this can be found in Huynh, H. Two simple classes of mastery scores based on the beta-binomial model. *Psychometrika,* 1977, *42,* 601-608.

more than once, consider the *entire period of its use* an opportunity to
collect validity information. Each administration is a chance to find out
more about the opinions of judges, the instrument's correlation with the
respondents' performance on other measures, and the performance of
criterion groups, as well as its concurrent and predictive validity, to be
discussed below. Establishing construct validity should be a continuing
process.

Approach 2. Descriptive Use of an Instrument: Content Validity

Before an instrument can be written to test for the presence of a particular
skill, the construct has to be translated into a set of distinctive *behaviors*.
These behaviors are described in terms of how people act, or occasionally,
what others tend to say about them. The test itself is then constructed in
order to prompt people to display these characteristic behaviors.

Now any complex construct, such as "effective writing ability," will be
definable as a collection of several *different* types of behavior; and its
accurate detection may even require using more than one kind of measurement instrument. Figure 5, for example, shows a collage of the behaviors
that you might decide would collectively indicate that someone writes
well.[20] Examining the figure should bring to mind any number of tasks
that could be included in tests of effective writing. A complete list of all
the relevant tasks would constitute an immense collection. Since no test
can encompass all of them, the actual instrument you construct must
contain a *sample* of the possible tasks. *Content validity refers to the
representativeness* of the sample of questions included in the instrument.
If a test is criterion-referenced and addressed to one or two subcomponents, then the test's content validity refers to how representatively its five
or so items represent the subconstructs it is intended to assess.

Content validity when a single test is supposed to represent a broad construct

To assure content validity a single general test of effective writing based on
Figure 5 would have to do two things. It should:

1. Include tasks that represent the use of skills from all seven categories of
   behavior to be presented.
2. Give *emphasis* to each category according to its importance in providing
   evidence of the construct, as depicted in the figure. In cases where the

---

20. For a test addressed to a large general subject area, this construct collage will
bear a strong resemblance to the test plan or content/process matrix described on
page 14. They are alternative ways of mapping the territory covered by the test.

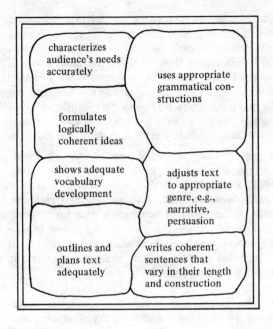

Figure 5. Hypothetical collage of categories of behaviors comprising the construct Effective Writing.
Categories providing stronger evidence of the construct have been assigned a proportionately larger
area.

construct to be measured can be divided into discrete and mutually
exclusive categories—say, for example, in measuring math skills—this
can be controlled by means of the number of questions asked per
category or the number of points earned by answering correctly the
questions from different categories.

When measuring *complex* skills such as writing—where skills are not
discrete and good performance means using different abilities all at once—
the task of assuring adequate representation is difficult. There are two
possible approaches to this task:

1. If the test of effective writing you plan to develop will depend on
   students' producing *writing samples*, then you can assure attention to
   the seven categories defining the construct by prescribing that readers

produce seven separate scores, one for each. These scores could then be *weighted* to produce a final composite test score based on the *proportional* contribution of each category to the overall construct. Looking at Figure 5, this means that "outlines and plans text . . . ," a particularly important skill, would be weighted more heavily than "shows adequate vocabulary . . . ," which takes up a smaller proportion of the graph. To make the differential weighting justifiable, however, you will need to assure that the test itself demands proportionately more organizational skill than vocabulary skill from the students—no small task!

2. You can circumvent the complicated problem of asking for seven separate scores, and then weighting them, by moving some of the more discrete skills to separate subtests. For instance, your instrument could include multiple-choice tests of vocabulary and grammar. This would limit to five the number of score categories for readers and perhaps make the task of scoring the test slightly easier. In determining the composite score, however, vocabulary and grammar subtest scores would be included with the others—again proportionate to their representation in the overall construct.

In most achievement testing situations, you will have less trouble accommodating the need for content validity. Consider, for example, the job of examining the content validity of a test to assess the effectiveness of a first-year algebra program. The construct, *first-year algebra,* might break down in a way similar to that shown in the construct collage at the left in Figure 6. Here units of instruction show relatively discrete and mutually exclusive category areas. Logarithms can be tested separately from quadratic equations; graphing, from positive and negative whole numbers. In this case, proper test emphasis can be controlled by means of the number of questions asked or the number of points assigned to each question in scoring. The test at the right in Figure 6 is content valid. Its high content validity means that the test "maps onto" the collection of possible questions that could be asked about this construct by sampling representatively from its various manifestations.

A measure that focuses too heavily on one category as in Figure 7 is not content valid for measuring the whole. It is content valid only for the categories it *does* measure. The test in Figure 7, for instance, would be more accurately titled "A Test For Quadratic Equations with a Few Logarithms Thrown In."

Content validity when criterion-referenced tests represent subconstructs

A test developer building a criterion-referenced test battery for the first year algebra course depicted in Figure 6 would approach the problem of

Figure 6. Construct collage for first-year algebra course with front page of a test seeking to have *good content validity*—that is, to proportionately represent each component category of the construct as depicted by the collage. Note that larger categories receive greater emphasis on the test.

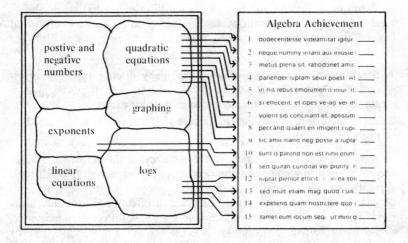

Figure 7. Construct collage for first-year algebra course with achievement test showing poor content validity. The category "quadratic equations" is over-represented, some categories are under-represented, and some are excluded altogether.

content validity[21] a little differently from her colleague constructing a single general test. First of all, the battery builder can construct a *separate test* for each discrete behavior category, so she need not worry about proportionate representation. *Her* concern related to content validity will be *that each test she writes reflect its own category and only its category.* Whereas the general test developer must be concerned that the test's items proportionately represent different, *heterogeneous* behaviors comprising the construct, the development of a single highly-specific test needs to ensure sameness, or *homogeneity,* of items. *Representativeness of a criterion-referenced test means that all its items reflect the same particular skill or skills.*

Now the algebra course unit on "positive and negative numbers" likely can be broken down to quite a few *yet-more-specific* skills such as addition and subtraction of negative numbers, inverse operations, multiplication and division, absolute values. Each of these is distinct enough to make necessary its own separate test. In the interest of content validity, such precise specification of additional separate tests may be necessary. It ensures that each test measures *only* what it says it does.

As you might have imagined, the need for item homogeneity makes construction of CRTs difficult for complex constructs such as effective writing. An initial temptation might be to define the construct as a thousand small abilities and test all of them! But such a test would almost surely lose its construct validity for describing skills needed in the world beyond the test. The best current solution to the problem of CRTs for complex skills is to

1. Break down the complex area into as many discrete types of performance as you can, say, writing letters, short narratives, arguments, etc.—and try to create separate uniform tests for each.
2. Score these tests according to separate skill categories, as described on pages 97 and 98.

A word needs to be said about the accuracy of the construct collages used as a basis for guiding construction of content valid tests. Since little is currently known about the psychological processes contributing to complex skills such as creative problem solving or effective writing, educators must remain uncertain about which behaviors best reflect their existence. A picture of "effective writing" such as the one in Figure 5, while it might rest on best guesses about the degree of contribution of different abilities to the overall construct, must remain supposition. There is no neat photo

---

21. Popham (1978, p. 155) prefers to call this *descriptive* validity. He suggests two methods for defending validity of criterion-referenced measures: judgments by raters of item homogeneity and criterion-group tryouts.

of the psyche to serve as the basis for test construction. Thus, test builders must either rely on hunches or use fairly technical analytic procedures to define the constructs they aim to assess.[22]

When you attempt to assess the content validity of your own or purchased instruments, the best thing to do is to create for yourself your own mental construct collage and assure yourself that the test or the test battery (1) has not left out any important behaviors, and (2) contains the proper proportion of items representing each sub-area of potential behaviors.

Some attempt should be made to demonstrate construct and content validity whenever you discuss the use of an instrument that is intended to describe *how much* of a skill people possess. You will notice that neither form of validity is easy to determine. The best way to describe a test's validity in your report will be to make a list of the *possible challenges* that might be made to its appropriateness for the particular situation, and to marshal the information you have assembled to answer each of them in turn.

Approach 3. Descriptive Use of an Instrument: Concurrent Validity

The concurrent validity of an instrument is established by collecting data to see if the results obtained with the instrument agree with results from other instruments, administered at approximately the same time, to measure the same thing. Let us say, for example, that you have administered a reading pretest to students in a new remedial program. At the same time, the program teachers gave each student an oral reading test which yielded a composite score based on reading fluency, speed, and comprehension. If the reading test and the teachers' oral measures yielded essentially the same results—the same students scored high or low on both measures—then the measures, in effect, have supported each other's validity. Calculating concurrent validity is useful in two situations:

1. Some circumstances call for a relatively *quick* estimate of the state of people's achievement. Concurrent validity is often calculated on a measure that someone has developed in order to shorten the time spent testing. In the reading test example above, the written reading test will save a considerable amount of teacher time and produce similar results.
2. A demonstration that a test has concurrent validity is good evidence of its construct validity. If it gives you results similar to those from

22. For an in-depth discussion of methods for systematically breaking down constructs in preparation for testing, see Guttman, L. Integration of test design and analysis. In *Proceedings of the 1969 Invitational Conference on Testing Problems,* pp. 53-65. Princeton, NJ: Educational Testing Service, 1970.

another test, and that test's validity for measuring a particular construct has been fairly well established, then you can build a case that your test also measures the construct. This use of correlational evidence to establish validity is discussed on page 94 .

Concurrent validity is determined by calculating a correlation coefficient between results from the instrument in question and results for the same individuals on a different measure of similar or related behavior, where both sets of results are taken to represent the status of the individuals during the same period of time. This correlation statistic is then recorded and discussed in the evaluation report. For some pointers about setting up data for calculating a correlation coefficient, see page 110.

Concurrent validity is often calculated for norm-referenced tests; but since criterion-referenced tests usually fail to provide the amount of score variability necessary for correlations, concurrent validity of criterion-referenced tests is seldom discussed.

Approach 4. Decision Related Use of an Instrument: Predictive Validity

Construct, content, and concurrent validity are concerned with how well an instrument represents a person's possession of a certain construct—a skill, attitude, or ability. It often happens that test developers care little about exactly *what* a test measures, preferring to define its value in terms of its ability to *predict future behavior*. For these situations, developers have employed methods for determining predictive validity.

If, for example, students who receive high scores on a high school exit exam later show high achievement in college, one could say that the exit exam distinguishes among those who will or will not do well in pursuing higher education. The test might be used subsequently with comparable accuracy to make similar predictions. Predictive, like concurrent validity, can be calculated and expressed as a *correlation coefficient* relating the instrument in question to a valid measure of the later-occurring predicted behavior.

Predictive validity of a criterion-referenced test could be shown by statistically comparing later performances of people who had either passed or failed it. A test battery's predictive validity might be computed by correlating overall raw score of number of objectives passed with measures of later performance.

In the best of all possible worlds, each applicable kind of validity would be assessed each time an instrument was used. Rarely is the validity question so thoroughly attacked, however. You will have to be the judge of how much time and effort you can devote to establishing the validity of the instruments you use. Your evaluation report should frankly note validity problems that have to be left unresolved.

Threats To Validity

The following are reasons why efforts to produce valid achievement tests might fail:

1. *Lack of objectivity or standardization in test administration.* You will remember that test validity depends not only upon the contents of the test but also on *the conditions under which it is administered.* You need to ensure that your test is given in the same way in classroom B as it was in classroom A. To the extent that you allow the method of administration to remain *unprescribed,* you increase the likelihood that its administrator will feel free to introduce instructions or changes, give help or hints, or allow too much time to some students. All of these will differentially bias the results.

2. *Response bias or evaluation apprehension.* Response bias refers to a situation in which people taking a test develop a strategy for responding based on something other than their knowledge of the subject matter. The test constructor, for example, may have made the error in a multiple choice test of making "A" the correct answer too often; or perhaps students have noticed that the correct answer is the option with the largest number of words. Tests with built-in response bias measure skill in taking tests—not the construct in question. Evaluation apprehension refers to the anxiety many people experience when taking a test for a life-guiding decision. In program evaluation, if the test results will be used for judging only the program and not the individual student, you should reassure respondents. It is not a good idea, on the other hand, to allow achievement test takers to remain anonymous. This removes a certain amount of motivation to do well and take the test seriously.

3. *Too few items per objective.* Sometimes achievement tests aimed at assessing a broad range of achievements rely on one or two questions to detect the presence of a particular skill. A single item is open to myriad errors not only in interpretation but also in computing or formulating a response. The skeptic can always challenge results from single items on the grounds of indeterminate effects from both random and purposeful errors. Although the *test as a whole* may be a valid measure of achievement in the *general* subject area it represents, you will be unable to make a valid judgment about the presence of the particular subskill measured by only one item.

4. *Tests that measure the skill too narrowly.* Sometimes the inference made from a test score applies to a broader range of abilities than is justified by the comparatively *restricted* nature of the actual test items. A test of ability to *write* that focuses only on paragraphs, for example, is not a valid indicator of ability to write themes. A test that demands

addition of fractions with a common denominator does not indicate ability to add fractions when the denominators are different.

5. *Mismatch between the skills called for by the test and the stated objective of the test.* A test, for instance, that requires students to mark an X over words spelled incorrectly does not measure attainment of the objective that students be able to spell the words themselves. Such a test should not, in fact, be called a spelling test if your audience is likely to interpret the results as indicating students' ability to spell words correctly from memory.

6. *Tests whose format and wording are tied to the idiosyncracies of a particular set of instructional materials.* Such tests, often "embedded" within a set of instructional materials, tap to some extent students' mastery of the formats used by the particular materials. For example, students may be instructed to add with materials using a horizontal format—$x + y =$ —rather than a vertical format $\begin{array}{r} x \\ + y \\ \hline \end{array}$. Since there is no way of knowing *how much* the knowledge of format affects performance, results of these tests are hard to interpret. In an evaluation using a control group, the use of tests embedded in one program is unfair to the students in the other program.

Summary

Remember that validity has to do with an instrument's appropriateness for accomplishing your purposes. These purposes might be to describe people or to make a decision about them, or both. If you wish to describe them, you want to discuss how much of a skill or ability they have. If you expect your audience to accept the results from an instrument used for this purpose, you need to demonstrate construct, content, or concurrent validity. Construct validity refers to how well the instrument measures what it claims to measure. Demonstrating construct validity demands clear definition of the construct, then presentation of logical arguments, credible opinions, and evidence from correlational or criterion group studies— all aimed at ruling out alternative explanations of the instrument's results. Content validity refers to how well the items give appropriate emphasis to the various components of the construct. To show content validity, you should provide evidence that the instrument contains a set of items which sample the construct's various sub-areas and give each its proportionate emphasis. If the test is criterion-referenced, content validity requires that its items be homogeneous. Concurrent validity is calculated when you use the result of one measure to predict the results of an alternative contemporaneous measure. Predictive validity justifies a test's usefulness for making decisions about people—such as selection for special programs. A case is usually made for predictive validity by demonstrating that the instrument correlates well with valid measures of the behavior it is intended to predict.

The credibility of your evaluation depends on the use of valid instruments. Since there is no established correct method for determining validity, when you select, construct, administer, and interpret your instruments, try to anticipate skepticism about your results; select appropriate methods for investigating possible criticisms; and finally, describe the precautions you have taken and the results of your validity investigation in your evaluation report.

Reliability: Does the Test Produce Consistent Results?

If you were to give students a math test one day and, without additional instruction, give them the same test two days later, you would expect each student to receive more or less the same score. If this should turn out *not* to be the case, you would have to conclude that your instrument is *unreliable,* because, without instruction, a person's knowledge of math does not fluctuate much from day to day. If the score fluctuates, then, the problem must be with the test. Its results must be influenced by things other than math knowledge. All these other things are called *error.* *Reliability refers to the extent to which measurement results are free of unpredictable kinds of error.*

Sources of error that affect reliability include:

- Fluctuations in the mood or alertness of respondents because of illness, fatigue, recent good or bad experiences, or other temporary differences among members of the group being measured.

- Variations in the conditions of administration from one testing to the next. These range from various distractions, such as unusual outside noise, to inconsistencies in the administration of the instrument, such as oversights in giving directions.

- Differences in scoring or interpreting results, chance differences in what an observer notices, and errors in computing scores.

- Random effects by examinees or respondents who guess or check off alternatives without trying to understand them.

Methods for demonstrating an instrument's reliability—whether the instrument is a long and general one or is composed of just a few items—involve comparison of one administration with another administration *to the same people.* This is followed by calculation of a statistic that measures relationships (usually a correlation coefficient) to demonstrate the similarity of two sets of results. The higher the correlation, the smaller the influence of error. Unlike validity, reliability is expressed as a number, usually a *reliability coefficient,* which is a positive decimal less than 1. Like validity, reliability has a long history; and several methods for demonstrating it have evolved. Which one is used will depend partly on the characteristics of the instrument and partly, as usual, on availability of resources such as money and time.

Test-retest reliability is the oldest and most intuitively obvious method for demonstrating instrument consistency. It involves the basic readministration method described above. Readministration must occur, however, within a time period during which the ability, attitude, or skill cannot itself be expected to change. For measuring most constructs, a good rule-of-thumb has been to wait a month between administrations. Readministration to the same group within a few days or weeks presents a problem: How much of what they remember from the first administration has carried over to the second? Even waiting a month does not eliminate this potential challenge, though it reduces its potency. A long time between administrations, on the other hand, raises the possibility that the "true" skill or attitude of the respondents will have changed. In order to divorce reliability measures from either memory effects or real changes, other methods of detecting reliability have been developed.

Alternate-form reliability attacks the problem of memory effects upon the second administration by having the developer write two essentially equivalent forms of the same instrument.[23] Each individual who receives form A on the first occasion will later receive form B, and vice versa. The method does not completely eliminate the effects of memory, since format across forms remains the same, however; and it does demand that time be spent writing extra items and typing two test forms. In cases where two forms of an instrument have been planned anyway, this kind of check on the reliability of locally produced instruments should be considered.

Split-half reliability yields a measure of test consistency within a single administration.[24] It allows the developer to obtain the two necessary scores from the same group of people by taking two halves of the items comprising an instrument and treating them as two administrations. Thus it separates reliability considerations from the effects of learning or developmental change on the respondents. It compares two forms of the test (the two halves) worked on as simultaneously as is humanly possible! Calculating split-half reliability demands, of course, that the questions that

---

23. This is usually done by writing several versions—as alike as possible—of the same item and then randomly assigning half to each test form.

24. It is not useful to calculate split-half reliability for criterion-referenced tests which have only five or so items.

comprise the two halves be as alike as possible. Otherwise, your calculation of the effect of error will be complicated by a change in real content.[25] Because of this, the split-half method for estimating reliability is best used with instruments that have many items, and where pairs of items can be considered equivalent enough for random distribution to essentially separate forms. These conditions are more likely to be met by items on a test with homogeneous items—like a general vocabulary test—than by items on a test of a complex skill like poetry writing or even reading. Then, too, split-half reliability yields a rather specialized sort of information. It tells you whether subgroups of the items on the test yield essentially the same results. A high split-half correlation means that the test is *internally consistent*, to use the nicely descriptive measurement jargon. Internal consistency, which can be measured in several ways other than split-half correlation, refers to the tendency of different items to elicit the same ability or attitude from any given respondent on a single administration of the instrument. It is important to remember, however, that measures of internal consistency do *not* tell you about error that might result from taking the test on different occasions. For this reason, they are *not* a good way to demonstrate reliability if you need to present a case that the instrument is consistent across administrations. Calculations of split-half reliability, in addition, should be supplemented by a statistical adjustment to correct for the small size of the two item pools being compared. Most statistics texts describe this procedure.

Inter-rater Reliability

Special problems for establishing reliability arise when the "instrument" is actually a *person*, for example, an observer, interviewer or reader of essay questions. The fact that the perceptions of this person can fluctuate leads to doubts about the accuracy of these measures. Not only may the test environment and the behavior of the person who is being tested vary from time to time; the *perceptions* of the people doing the reporting might diverge as well. That is, two people looking at the same sample of behavior may rate it differently, and the *same* person looking at the *same* sample at different times may arrive at different ratings. The reader of an essay question, for example, might see an answer as indicating "excellent" comprehension of the topic at time *A* and only "average" at time *B*.

The best way to demonstrate that your evaluation has been minimally contaminated by inconsistency among "human instruments" is to *have more than one person* perform at least a sample of the observations or the readings that the test requires. If different people report behavior or

---

25. This necessity, if you think about it, makes split-half reliability similar to alternate-form reliability with both forms administered at the same time.

activities in essentially the same way, then you have evidence that the rules for recording have been well learned and uniformly applied by the principal observer or rater.

If your test uses essay questions, and only a *single* reader, you can estimate this person's reliability in the following way:

Train *another person,* who will act as a reliability check, to score the essays in the same way as the principal reader. Then have this person read and rate a representative sample of the essays. The reliability coefficient which you are able to calculate by correlating scores from these two readers will give you an idea of the consistency with which your one observer can be counted on to score the essays accurately.

Incidentally, if you will be able to have *more than one reader or observer score each essay or event* during data collection, it is good practice to include in your evaluation report the *mean* of the scores given by these separate raters. Because this information comes from several sources, it will be more reliable than separate scores.

Precisely *how* to calculate inter-rater reliability is at present a question whose answer is long and rich in contingencies. Because the issue is difficult to resolve, your best strategy will be to

- Focus your defense of the measurement method on its *validity.* If you can present good evidence that scoring via raters is appropriate for obtaining accurate information, then the issue of reliability will become moot.

- Have a data analyst examine your situation, and then recommend and perform an appropriate test of inter-rater reliability.

Table 8 shows a data display for organizing score results from two raters in preparation for calculating a coefficient of inter-rater reliability. The table directs you to compare two judges' answers to each of an instrument's "items." Down the left-hand column, you should list the items on the instrument. X should be Rater X's responses to the item; Y should be Rater Y's. In some cases, the instrument in question might not contain responses to *items* as such. Readers of essays, for example, might produce ranks or ratings per essay, or even narrative critiques. In these cases, your data analyst will help you find the best solution for completing the table.

If you have only *two* observers, and their ratings will be based on just a few specific criteria rather than demand complicated decisions, then you can probably compute inter-rater reliability from the table by means of a *correlation.* A high correlation (roughly .70 or above) shows that the measurement method is sufficiently reliable. Lower correlations indicate

TABLE 8
Data Display To Begin Calculating
Inter-rater Reliability

Instrument Items	Rater or Observer X	Rater or Observer Y
1		
2		
3		
4		
5		
6		
7		
etc.		

that the observers or reporters do not agree about what they are reporting, and you should be correspondingly skeptical about the data you receive.

Recently, some authors have nominated a correlation-like statistic, Cohen's Kappa,[26] as a substitute for more standard correlation coefficients when calculating inter-rater reliabilities with data from ranks or ratings. Kappa is easy to calculate and interpret, but only if data have been entered into the equation properly. For this, once more, you will need a data analyst.

If you will use *more than two* observers or raters, *or* if your two raters will be required to make decisions using multiple criteria, *or* if they will record many different features of what they see, then it might be appropriate to estimate inter-rater reliability using analysis of variance (ANOVA) rather than a correlation.[27] Since the exact form of ANOVA you use will depend on your situation, and since the best way to perform the ANOVA is by computer, you should consult a data analyst to help you in this case.

---

26. Description of Cohen's Kappa can be found in Cohen, J. A coefficient of agreement for nominal scales. *Educational and Psychological Measurement,* 1960, *20,* 37-46. Also see Fleiss, J. L. *Statistical methods for rates and proportions.* New York: John Wiley & Sons, 1973.

27. Analysis of variance is discussed briefly in Fitz-Gibbon, C. T., & Morris, L. L. How to design a program evaluation. In L. L. Morris (Ed.), *Program evaluation kit.* Beverly Hills: Sage Publications, 1978. A discussion of the use of ANOVA for the specific purpose of estimating inter-rater reliability can be found in Ebel, R. L. Estimation of the reliability of ratings. *Psychometrika,* 1951, 16, 407-424. See also Medley, D. M., & Mitzel, H. E. Application of analysis of variance to the estimation of the reliability of observations of teachers' classroom behavior. *Journal of Experimental Education,* 1958, *27,* 23-25.

Determining the Reliability of Tests Which You Construct Yourself

Determining the reliability of your own tests requires that you calculate a statistic such as a correlation that shows the relationship between different administrations of the instrument or among items on the instrument at a single administration.

Calculating any correlation coefficient involves setting up the results from various administrations of instruments according to Table 9. You will notice that the columns are labeled X and Y. Column X refers to one administration of an instrument. Column Y refers to another. If you are calculating reliability, X is administration 1, Y is administration 2. (If you were calculating concurrent or predictive *validity*, then X would be the instrument which you were validating, and Y would be the instrument which you were using as a criterion.) Listed down the left-hand column are student's names. While you need not refer to people by name, the lefthand column should contain some listing of individuals to whom both administrations have been given. In order to array data for calculating a correlation, simply list the scores on the various measures attained by each person. Then use a standard statistics text to choose the correlation coefficient appropriate to the type of data the tests have generated.[28]

TABLE 9
Data Display To Begin Calculating
a Correlation Coefficient

Names	X	Y
Evans, E.		
Handler, H.		
Kendall, K.		
Lee, L.		
Norris, N.		
Olsen, O.		
Ryan, R.		
Sanford, S.		
Turner, T.		
Weston, W.		

28. See, for example, Fitz-Gibbon, C. T., & Morris, L. L. How to calculate statistics. In L. L. Morris (Ed.), *Program evaluation kit*. Beverly Hills: Sage Publications, 1978.

If you plan to calculate a reliability coefficient for *your own* tests, the following pointers, based on previous experience of test developers, will help you increase the likelihood of obtaining a high coefficient.

Suggestion 1. Beware that calculating a correlation coefficient may give you an inaccurate estimate of reliability

Determining a reliability coefficient for a test usually means calculating a correlation between its two administrations. The size of correlation is affected by the *variability* of the *scores* obtained. In other words, if a test is reliable, then the results from administration A and administration B are most likely to show a high correlation *if both administrations have produced a wide range of values.* This is so because all measurement is subject to error; and if there is very little difference among the scores of different people (i.e., low variability), then only a little error will be required to render a person's standing at administration B different from her standing at administration A.

In computing reliabilities of long, general, usually norm-referenced tests, you can promote high score variability by (1) including a wide range of different skill levels among the people cooperating in the reliability study, (2) using a large sample, and (3) manipulating some characteristic of the test. These strategies render *correlation* an appropriate reliability check with long tests of general skills or aptitudes. In the case of criterion-referenced tests, however, low score variability can be common. This is because any one criterion-referenced test is usually short, allowing a range of scores across perhaps only five items. What is more, such tests are constructed so that everyone who has the skill in question will receive high scores. People will either score high and pass them or fail them outright. For this reason, most writers on the subject of the technical quality of criterion-referenced tests recommend checks on the reliability of the *decisions* made about people using these tests rather than scores received. A reliability study of this sort would require setting up the results of two test administrations as in Table 10. One of several statistical techniques can then be used to determine whether the pass-fail pattern shown in the table could have occurred by chance.[29] If a fair degree of relationship appears to exist between decisions based on the two administrations, then the test is reliable.

---

29. A phi coefficient or a Chi-square test come first to mind, but these might give too low an estimate of relationship. Some statisticians recommend *Cohen's Kappa* for determining relationships among measures placing scores into categories. See footnote 26 for this reference. It should be noted that a criterion-referenced test can place scores into *more than two* categories; that is, Table 10 could have had additional cells—for instance, Pass/Needs remediation/Fail. Cohen's Kappa handles these situations as well.

TABLE 10
Number of Persons Passing and Failing
a Criterion-Referenced Test
on Two Administrations

		ADMINISTRATION 1	
		Passed	Failed
	Passed	45	14
ADMINIS-TRATION 2			
	Failed	4	56

Suggestion 2. Conduct an item analysis as a means of increasing test reliability

The purpose of an item analysis is to point out items that tend to reduce the scores of respondents who score high or to raise the scores of respondents who score low. In other words, item analysis helps you to find items which, for one reason or another, are inappropriate to the test, so that they can be removed or changed. Poor items lower reliability by reducing score variability or the homogeneity of criterion-referenced test items. Because of this, of course, they also make the test less valid.

Statistical techniques of item analysis are described in most measurement texts for making comparisons between how respondents performed on individual items and how they scored on the instrument as a whole. You can perform an *informal* item analysis by the method illustrated in this example:

Example. The first draft of a general science achievement test containing 65 items has been administered to 80 students. Twenty high and 20 low scorers, that is, the top and bottom 25 percent of the 80 students, have been identified. The completed instruments from these 40 students are examined, and the responses to each item are summarized in Table 11.

The table's columns name the possible scores for each item, in this case, pass or fail. The rows list the items. By placing in one pile the responses of high scorers (those whose total score fell in the upper 25% range) and in a second pile the responses of low scorers (those whose total score fell in the lower 25% range), the evaluator can make a quick tally of how the people in each of the groups scored on each item.

TABLE 11
Tallies of Pass/Fail Patterns Per Item
for the 20 Highest and Lowest Scorers
on a General Science Test

Item No.	20 highest scorers' scoring pattern		20 lowest scorers' scoring pattern	
	Pass	Fail	Pass	Fail
1	///	卌 卌 卌 //	卌 卌 卌 卌	
2	卌 卌 卌 //	///	卌 卌 卌 ///	//
3	卌 卌 卌	卌	卌 /	卌 卌 ////
4	卌 卌 卌 ///	//	///	卌 卌 卌 //

etc.
to 65

This is what the table tells you:

- If the test will be used to *select* students for a program, you may want to shorten the test a great deal while retaining those items that most high scorers get right and that most low scorers tend to fail. In this case, you would discard items 1, 2, and 3 but retain item 4.

- If the test is criterion-referenced, then you will want to look at item 1 closely to find out what went wrong. Can you see by examining the item why the high scorers on this test usually got the first item wrong and why the low scorers passed it? The second item appears to have been easy for all but a few students. Was the objective measured by this item an easy objective, was there a "giveaway" element to the item, or was the objective just so well taught that the results reflect effective instruction? You may have to interview some students whose performance on particular items is puzzling. Thus, for measuring achievement via a criterion-referenced test, the only item that is clearly "misfiring" is item 1. Which of the other items to retain for a CRT should be based on factors other than their power to discriminate high from low scorers.

Suggestion 3. Try to build the reliability and validity tests into your assessment plan so that they present minimal inconvenience to yourself and the program staff

If you have little reason to doubt the validity of the test, you can use the results from its "official administration" as part of a reliability or validity check. For instance, you might randomly choose a group of respondents and administer the test to this group twice—once, at the time of data collection, and perhaps three weeks before or after. The calculation of relationship for the random group between these two administrations is your check on reliability.   A *validity* study could proceed in much the same way. The criterion against which your test is to be validated—another achievement test, classroom performance, or teacher rating—could be administered to a sample of your respondents at roughly the same time as the administration of your test.

Reliability and the Measurement of Complex Achievements

Some guidance about what constitutes high and low reliability in instruments you choose to use is in order, since repeated reference is made to them in this chapter. Reliability coefficients of .70 or above are usually considered respectable, regardless of the type of reliability calculated or the method of calculation used; and coefficients of .90 and above are not unusual for standardized achievement tests. In the case of tests aimed at assessing achievement of higher order or complex skills—such as problem solving, creativity, good writing, and various measures of on the job performance—reliability coefficients tend to be somewhat lower. This is because these measures often rely upon the scoring of real life performances; and unless the scoring method has been elaborately detailed and used with highly trained scorers and observers, reliability tends to suffer. While reliability coefficients of .70 are certainly desirable among such measures, lower coefficients are sometimes tolerated, although this could affect the confidence with which you can make decisions based on test results.

If only tests of doubtful reliability are available to you, consider the amount of time and effort it takes to administer, score, and interpret them, and the amount of inconvenience they cause for respondents. The more resources an instrument demands, the more you should hesitate to use it if its reliability is low. A less reliable test is less likely to reveal the *real difference* that you hope the program makes. On the other hand, if you have the necessary time, and you are not overly burdening the respondents, an additional measure might provide you with good hunches about program effects.

Low reliability poses a particular kind of disadvantage for program evaluation. You are using the instruments, after all, to monitor the effectiveness of a program. Typically this means comparing one group mean with another, say two groups receiving different programs, or the same program at different times. Because the error associated with low reliability is random, that error will tend to affect both administrations. It will *not* systematically bias the results in favor of or against either administration. What low reliability will do is blur the difference between the two group measures. It is as if the instrument were trying to give you a message about program effectiveness, but its low reliability introduced static into your reception. If the message gets through anyway, then the low reliability poses no problem. The difficulty is that when the reliability is low, you may not get the message at all. Your statistical test is more likely to register "no significant difference" as a result of increased variance due to error (as opposed to good variance due to the construct) on each measure. And if this is the result of your study, apologizing for the low reliability of the instrument is likely to sound like Monday-morning quarterbacking—a poor substitute for favorable results.

The need for high test reliability in *program* studies is, however, less crucial than when you are making decisions about individuals. The reason is that statistical bases for *selecting* individuals according to relative standing on a measure are directly related to reliability. In such a situation, you are primarily concerned with purely statistically-based predictive validity. In program evaluation, your primary concern is with construct validity and content validity. These, as you have seen, can be demonstrated by methods other than correlations.

For Further Reading

Anastasi, A. *Psychological testing.* New York: Macmillan, 1968.

Cronbach, L. J. Test validation. In R. L. Thorndike (Ed.), *Educational measurement.* Washington, D.C.: American Council on Education, 1970.

Fitz-Gibbon, C. T., & Morris, L. L. How to calculate statistics. In L. L. Morris (Ed.), *Program evaluation kit.* Beverly Hills: Sage Publications, 1978.

Hambleton, R. K. et al. Criterion-referenced testing and measurement: A review of technical issues and developments. *Review of Educational Research*, 1978, *48*(1), 1-47.

Mehrens, W. A., & Lehmann, I. J. *Measurement and evaluation in education and psychology.* New York: Holt, Rinehart and Winston, 1973.

Mehrens, W. A., & Lehmann, I. J. *Standardized tests in education.* New York: Holt, Rinehart and Winston, 1975.

Popham, W. J. *Criterion-referenced measurement.* New Jersey: Prentice-Hall, 1978.

Talmage, H. *Statistics as a tool for educational practitioners.* Berkeley: McCutchan Publishing, 1976.

Chapter 6

Using Achievement Test Data

Once the achievement test you have selected or designed has been administered, you face the task of organizing the information and extracting what is relevant for your use. You must use the data to judge how well the program—or an experimental treatment if you are conducting a short experiment—has achieved its intended objectives. However, you might also want to characterize the program or its participants in any number of other ways, possibly calculating correlations to show relationships among achievement and student or program characteristics. The suggestions provided by this chapter will help you to work with the achievement scores you obtain and to complete the following tasks:

- Recording data from achievement measures which you have constructed
- Preparing what you will report about the program by calculating statistics and displaying results

Recording Data From Achievement Measures Which You Have Contructed

Purchased tests often come with scoring services. You, of course, will have to arrange your own scoring for tests constructed by yourself or the program staff. If your test scoring task is a large one, you might be able to lease or purchase a scoring machine. Sales representatives from data processing companies can provide you with sales and rental information.

Before you can interpret the scores, you may have to record the data from the tests onto a data summary sheet. Some achievement tests yield a single number—either the total number of items answered correctly or the total number of points earned. In some situations, however, you will want to know how well students performed on *subtests* or on *groups of items* measuring the same objectives. To separately score subparts of a test, you will need to record data on a summary sheet like the one in Figure 8 which shows a common sense way of tallying students' correct responses by objective.

Student	Objective 1 Items: M=4/5 1,6,12,15,19		Objective 2 Items: M=3/3 3,9,10		Objective 3 Items: M=5/6 5,14,18 points	
	Score	M	Score	M	Score	M
Barker, B.	4	+	2	0	3	0
Collins, C.	3	0	0	0	5	+
Dawson, D.	5	+	2	0	6	+
Drew, N.	1	0	2	0	4	0
Engel, E.	5	+	2	0	4	0

Figure 8. Data summary sheet for scoring an achievement test objective-by-objective. See text for explanation.

Student names are listed down the left-hand side of the data summary sheet. Objectives are listed across horizontally, at the head of columns, identified by number. Each objective has two columns. In the first column, you record the raw score on the items addressing the objective. The M at the head of the second column stands for mastery; criteria for mastery of each objective are listed as, for instance, M=4/5—a fraction in the cell naming the objective. In the second column, you record a + or a 0, depending on whether the raw score has met the mastery criterion. Students Dawson and Engle got all the items correct for Objective 1; student Barker had one wrong answer, but the four out of five criterion determined that a + be put in Barker's M column also. You will notice that the method for recording scores for Objective 1 "loses" information about the student's success with individual items. Most analyses you perform, however, will not require item-by-item information.

No student achieved the three out of three mastery criterion for Objective 2.

Items for Objective 3 are scored somewhat differently. For each of these items, a student can receive either *one or two points*. Though the subtest has three items, six points can be earned. The score column for Objective 3 contains the total number of points earned over the three items.

Graph paper, or the kind of paper used for computer programming, is useful for constructing these data summary sheets even when the data are to be processed by hand rather than by computer.

Summary Sheets For Computer Analyses

If a computer analyzes your data, then your data summary task will involve coding responses or arranging response sheets in preparation for keypunching.[30] *Coding sheets* for setting up a file of your results for the computer can either follow the format of the data summary sheet in Figure 8 or record each student's scores item by item. The latter is probably wiser since you could decide later to use item-by-item information—perhaps to correlate test scores with some other student characteristic or to conduct item analyses, as described on pages 112 and 113.

When achievement data are keypunched, entries for each examinee will become a separate card or a span of tape; but tapes simply condense and store data from cards. The standard card has 80 columns, so you can fit up to 80 pieces of single-digit information about each student on a card. The meaning of the digit in each column of the card is defined by a *codebook* written by the data analyst. Data coding is accomplished by punching holes over the numbers in the 80 card columns. When there is information to fill more than 80 columns, a second card is simply inserted behind the first card in the data deck.

Mechanical data processing, including computer analyses of data and perhaps even *machine scoring of test answer forms*, will affect the form of your data summary sheet or perhaps even make it unnecessary to have one. Since computer analyses and machine-scored testing are becoming easily accessible to schools and districts, you can perhaps conserve your own time by investigating these services. Call your district Research and Evaluation office or a few local data processing companies. If you find that mechanical data processing fits your time constraints and budget, then your data summary sheet will need to conform to the machine's requirements. You might even find that the student's answer sheet if formatted properly can be *read* and *scored* by a machine or that you can use a machine-scorable answer sheet. You might also persuade the district to adopt a general purpose machine-scorable answer sheet, like the one in Figure 9, to save time for everyone who must process test scores fast and accurately. In any case, if you plan to use machine scoring or computer data processing, discuss the format and content of your tests with your data analyst before you produce them en masse.

---

30. Basic texts containing additional information on data processing are available. One such book is Feingold's *Introduction to data processing*. Dubuque, Iowa: Wm. C. Brown, 1975. If you will be using the *Statistical Package for the Social Sciences* (SPSS), you might consult Fitz-Gibbon, C. T., & Morris, L. L. How to calculate statistics. In L. L. Morris (Ed.), *Program evaluation kit*. Beverly Hills: Sage Publications, 1978.

Figure 9. General purpose machine scorable answer sheet

What To Report About the Program

Norm- and criterion-referenced tests produce myriad types of scores. Depending on what your audience wants to know, these scores can be used to perform many analyses. It is likely that the questions your evaluation is supposed to answer—those which have guided you all along—will decide what sorts of achievement scores you collect and how you analyze and report them.

To suggest what you might do with achievement test scores, this section describes the types of scores that tests produce and explains some of the analyses that can be performed to answer different evaluation questions.

Types of Scores

Before you attempt to interpret a set of scores, you should understand what they can and cannot tell you. You may encounter three major types of achievement test scores:

- Raw scores
- Scores from criterion-referenced tests
- Scores from norm-referenced tests

Raw scores

Raw scores are aptly named. They are the first summary numbers you obtain when you score tests. They are computed prior to any conversion process introducing norms or performance standards. The most common raw score is the total number of items answered correctly. With tests that assign a different number of points to different items, the raw score is the total number of points earned. On timed tests, the raw score could be the speed with which the task has been done. Number of errors is another form of raw score. At times when speed and accuracy are important, such as in typing, the raw score usually includes both a determination of time elapsed and number of errors.

Whether you construct the test yourself or use a published one, you have the option of reporting raw scores and using them in your data analyses. Even if tests are to be sent away for scoring, you may want to score them yourself in order to get the raw score data early. Some test publishers provide scoring stencils so that you can calculate a quick score before the tests are sent away. You may also need to compute raw scores yourself if you want results from *groups of items* on the test rather than the entire test. Often the computer printout you receive from the publisher will report individual raw scores and averages along with corresponding percentiles and other norm scores.

Though raw scores out of context are hard to interpret, they are not meaningless. Raw scores are directly interpretable, for instance, in domain-referenced tests where you can clearly describe what it is the test measures. Raw scores, because they are most directly derived from the test, are, in addition, the appropriate numbers to be used when calculating statistics. T-tests, for instance, or analyses of variance, computed to determine whether there is a difference in average score between a program and control group, should be based on average raw scores, *not on converted scores.*

Criterion-referenced scores

Criterion-referenced scores are, of course, the scores obtained from criterion-referenced tests. An important feature of these tests is the presence of a criterion-level or cut-off score which determines passing, mastery, or acceptable performance. Because criterion-referenced tests are concerned with mastery, the score for any individual student is expressed usually as a *dichotomous,* either-or, judgment: The student has *passed* the test, exceeding the cut-off score, or has *failed* to do so. Occasionally, criterion tests will categorize performance into three or more levels, such as poor performance, remediable performance, and passing.

There is at present a growing literature on the subject of establishing criterion and cut-off scores.[31] The question of how many correct, or what level of performance should constitute mastery or superior as opposed to mediocre performance is at present a popular one. The issue is particularly pressing because of growing interest in state proficiency testing for high school graduation.

Since an acceptable *program* must be effective with *groups* of students, you will usually need to present group results from criterion-referenced tests. When dealing with individuals, a criterion test gives you information only about success or failure at passing a particular objective or meeting a certain proficiency standard. Quite a few methods are available for summarizing this pass-fail information in order to describe the performance of *groups.* The different approaches you can take with these summaries are discussed in a later section of the chapter beginning on page 133.

Norm-referenced scores

The norm scores available to you will nearly always reflect the performance of *individual students* as compared with other individuals. Norms

31. See, for instance, Hambleton, R. K., Swaminathan, H., Algina, J., & Coulson, D. B. Criterion-referenced testing and measurement: A review of technical issues and developments. *Review of Educational Research,* 1978, *48*(1), 1-47; and Swaminathan, H., Hambleton, R. K., & Algina, J. Reliability of criterion-referenced tests: A decision-theoretic formulation. *Journal of Educational Measurement,* 1974, *11,* 263-267.

may also be provided for classrooms, schools, or districts. Norm scores are often gathered as a result of a mandated state or district-wide testing program.

When norm-referenced tests are scored, the raw score for each student is converted to a norm-referenced percentile, stanine, or grade equivalent—a *standard* score which reflects the position of the raw score in comparison with members of the norm or standard *group*. Norm scores will be useful when you need to estimate for your audience how closely the performance of program participants matches that of a national or local norm group.

The most common norm scores are described in manuals accompanying published tests. Unlike statewide or local norms which reflect the rank of your school or students with respect to others in the same locality or of a similar background, norm score conversions provided by a test publisher are usually based on performance of some external norm or reference group. This external group is the set of students who were selected and tested by the test producers during the test's actual development—that is, during a certain month of a certain year, possibly some years ago. The reference or norm group is also called the standardization group. In fairness to the program you are evaluating, you want the standardization group to be representative of the students and grade levels it concerns.

The most common norm-referenced scores are these:

- *Percentiles* (also called centiles and percentile ranks), which show approximately what percent of students scored lower than a given raw score
- z-scores, T-scores, and other *linear standard scores*, which tell you how many standard deviations above or below the mean a given raw score has fallen
- T-scaled scores, stanines, and other *normalized standard scores*, which tell you *approximately* how many standard deviations above or below the mean a given raw score is, but are actually based on percentiles
- *Grade-equivalent scores*, which attempt to tell you what grade level— in years and months—typically corresponds to a given raw score. Because of the questionable manner in which they are derived, and because they are easily misinterpreted, grade equivalents should *not* be used as indicators of program performance.

Several sources containing detailed descriptions of the construction, scoring, and interpretation of norm-referenced tests are listed in For Further Reading, page 145.

Please note a common error that is made when norm scores are used to describe group performance: The mean of the individual norm scores from a group—say, a school—does *not* equal the norm score of the mean of the group. If, for instance, you administered the Comprehensive Test of Basic Abilities and calculated an average of the percentile scores of individual students, this number would *not* reflect the percentile of the school's average when compared to other schools. If the average percentile of the students in your school is 67, this does not mean that the school itself stands at the 67th percentile among schools.

In order to provide you with this information, the publisher would have to calculate the average raw score for each school using the CTBA and then compute a percentile ranking of *schools*. Few test developers do this. While the median percentile rank achieved by students in the school is a meaningful and useful number to report, be careful to inform your audiences that it might not accurately reflect the *school's* standing. Some state assessment programs do report school percentile rankings. This is usually the case when the state itself develops, administers, and norms the test. In this situation, the percentile that is reported reflects the actual standing of the school with respect to the other schools in the state.

Using Achievement Test Scores To Answer Common Evaluation Questions

This section discusses five questions that program evaluators usually find themselves answering or attempting to answer, namely:

- Which students should be placed in the program?
- How do the scores of program students compare with those of the control group?
- How do scores compare with past performance?
- To what extent have program objectives been obtained?
- Are achievement test results related to student characteristics or program variations?

In discussing the use of achievement scores in answering these questions, advice is given concerning the appropriate type or types of scores to use—criterion-referenced, norm-referenced, or raw scores. Some suggestions are also given with respect to reporting scores and using graphs and tables.

Question 1: Which students should be placed in the program?

It might occur that a funding agency has already prescribed the tests and cut-off scores to be used for selecting students to take part in, say, a gifted program. In this case, of course, the question of student placement has been answered for you. In other situations, however, you may have to make such determinations yourself.

How you decide which students should be in the program will depend on whether the program is intended for an "extreme" group—high or low performance—or whether the program students are supposed to be representative of students who span a range of abilities.

In selecting an extreme group to receive, for example, remedial instruction in math, you might opt to use either norm- or criterion-referenced tests. Your choice of test will be based on whether you want to select *a fixed number of participants who are most in need* or whether you wish to identify *everyone in need* as determined by a cut-off score. Say, for example, that there is room in a remedial class for only 20 students; then you will simply select the 20 students with the lowest scores. In this case, a norm-referenced test will probably serve you better because it draws fine distinctions among people with extreme strengths and deficiencies. Norm-referenced aptitude tests should also be considered if general ability is relevant to whether students are placed in a program.

If, on the other hand, the program intends to address a particular set of skills that all students are expected to learn, then criterion-referenced measures, with appropriate recommendations for cut-off scores, should help you identify every student who needs this instruction.

In some situations, you might want to select a program group that is *representative* of a large group of potential participants. This might occur, for instance, if you want to try out a pilot program with a small group before adopting it district-wide. To select a representative group, you should *graph raw scores* from whatever measure you deem most relevant for selecting program participants. Then, looking at the graph, see whether scores divide themselves into clusters or whether they form a smooth, almost continuous curve. Clusters of scores provide you with natural cut-off points; if the graph shows a smooth distribution, you will have to draw more arbitrary cut-off points between groups. After this, sample from each group or cluster so that the total program group contains high, middle, and low scorers in the same proportions as the larger group from which they are selected.

In some rare instances, you may be interested in choosing students for a program who have a specific skill deficiency, for instance, who cannot swim or who cannot take apart a carburetor. In these situations you will, of course, construct a criterion test which gives students a chance to display the particular skill.

Question 2: How do the scores of program students compare with those of the control group?

Your evaluation might use a control group design to allow you to estimate how program students might have achieved had they not taken part in the program. In such a case, you will want to compare achievement results from the two groups.

If the outcome measure is a norm-referenced test, then the best deter-
miner of comparative outcomes is a test for the statistical significance of
differences in the average *raw scores* from the groups on the test in
question. If just *two* groups are being compared, then a t-test for the
difference between means is probably the appropriate statistic. If more
than two are being compared, then an analysis of variance should be
performed. These techniques are described in most statistics books.[32]

TABLE 12
Pretest and Posttest Results
for Program Alpha and Program Beta Students

	N	Pretest (ability)			Posttest (Arithmetic)		
		Mean	SD	t-test of diff.	Mean	SD	t-test of diff.
Alpha	8	24.00	7.25	0.25	30.30	5.10	4.16*
Beta	14	24.86	7.12		15.80	8.60	

*statistically significant at the .05 level

Table 12 shows an example of how to report results of an evaluation
using a pretest-posttest design with a true-control group. The table for the
non-equivalent control group design is identical. Table 12 displays mean
raw scores for each program, the standard deviation associated with each
mean, and the t-test of the difference between means for both the pretest
and posttest. Note in this example that the pretest was a norm-referenced
ability test and the posttest was a norm-referenced *arithmetic* test. The
t-test for the difference between pretest scores was not significant. This is
indicated by the *absence* of an asterisk. This means that on the pretest the
two groups were more or less equivalent. If the difference between ability
test scores on the pretest had been significant, then the evaluator would
have been in trouble—the reason for using such a design is to show a
difference on the posttest scores between two groups which had initially
performed similarly. Having established that the groups were equivalent to
begin with, one then looks at results *after* the program, again by perform-

32. See Fitz-Gibbon, C. T., & Morris, L. L. How to calculate statistics. In L. L.
Morris (Ed.), *Program evaluation kit*. Beverly Hills: Sage Publications, 1978. A
description of the use of a true and non-equivalent control group designs can be
found in Fitz-Gibbon, C. T., & Morris, L. L. How to design a program evaluation, also
part of the *Program evaluation kit.*

ing a t-test on raw score means. The example shows a large difference between the posttest means. Not surprisingly, the t-test shows the difference to be significant, that is, bigger than could have been expected to occur by chance. For the example shown in Table 12, the evaluator can report:

> As was expected because of the use of random selection, the Alpha program and Beta control students were initially equivalent on the ability measure used as the pretest. After the program, however, the mean posttest score of the Alpha program students was significantly higher than the mean score of the Beta control group. This gain by Alpha students can be attributed to their participation in the program.

In addition to a table, raw score results from pretest and posttest can be displayed on a graph. Graphic representation is recommended because graphs are quickly understood and interpreted. In addition, graphs are almost always preferable when presenting results to a live audience. If the pre- and posttest were the *same* tests or an equivalent or parallel form of the same test, then using this kind of graph will always be appropriate:

Figure 10. Mean scores of the experimental group and control group on the pretest and posttest

If the pretest was *different* from the posttest—such as the ability test in Table 12—then display the posttest scores only. This is the simplest method of display and is acceptable if there was no significant difference between pretest scores:

Figure 11. Mean posttest scores of the
E-group and C-group

When interpreting results from a control group design study, remember the critical question:

Was the posttest mean for one group significantly different from the posttest mean for the other group?

It is not good procedure to test the difference between *group gains* from pretest to posttest. For statistical reasons, comparing gains usually penalizes the group whose pretest score was higher. Therefore, compare the scores between groups on either the pretest or posttest, *not* the differences in score *gains* from pretest to posttest.

When deciding whether observed differences in mean scores are *educationally* significant, confidence limits usually are a more useful statistic than the t-test. While a t-test of significance tells you whether the difference you have found is more than a chance difference, confidence limits give you an estimate of the range of differences you would find between experimental and control groups were you to repeat the study again and again. This range not only gives you an idea of how big the actual difference between the groups might be; it also permits a quick check on whether the difference obtained is significant.

If the mean posttest raw score is higher for the program group than for the control group, but not significantly different statistically, you might ask a data analyst to try a more powerful statistical test such as analysis of variance or analysis of covariance, discussed in most basic statistics tests.

If a battery of criterion-referenced tests has been used to determine the achievement of program and control group students, you can use a *total raw score* equal to the number of items correct on the whole battery to perform an analysis exactly the same as the one described here for norm-referenced tests. If, however, some objectives are more important than others, or if you wish to make interpretations of the test on an objective-by-objective basis, then statistical analyses of total scores will not give appropriate information for comparing the programs. What to do instead is discussed under Question 4 below.

Question 3: How do scores compare with past performance?

In the absence of a control group, you may wish to use achievement test results to express the results from a *time series design* or to document a change in the program group's performance *from pretest to posttest.* Such comparisons can take one of two forms. First, you can compare the achievement scores of a group with *their own previous scores* on the same measure or its equivalent form. A formative evaluator monitoring student progress, for instance, might give program students the same test periodically throughout the course of the program. A summative evaluator might decide to look at the program group's performance at last year's administration of the outcome measure—or perhaps over the last two years. In both cases, the measurement plan is said to be *longitudinal.* Pretest-posttest designs are always longitudinal.

In contrast, you might find it useful to employ a *successive groups design,* comparing current test results with past scores from *different* students who were then at the same developmental or grade level as those in the program. The successive groups design is often used in summative evaluations where a particular test is annually administered to a particular grade level.

When comparing changes in mean scores over time, whether with successive groups or longitudinally, you should use *raw scores* for both graphing and analysis.

Whether you choose to administer the *same* test over and again or to use equivalent forms is up to you. When using longitudinal and pretest-posttest designs, some evaluators prefer to administer *different* tests at each occasion to ensure against memory effects—learning of specific test items rather than generalized learning related to the objectives measured by the test. In order to eliminate item-specific memory effects, many test developers have created *parallel* or *alternate forms* of a test—with varying degrees of success.

You can check the degree of parallelism in tests you use in different ways. As evidence that different forms of a test will be parallel, *criterion-referenced test* developers rely on the care with which objectives have been described and the manner in which items have been sampled from the pool of potential items. You will have to use your judgment concerning a publisher's claims in this regard. You will find it easier to accept such descriptive evidence when dealing with tests of simple tasks, such as word-attack skills or arithmetic computation, than with tests of reading comprehension or other complex skills where specification of item types is looser. *Norm-referenced test* developers, on the other hand, are expected to provide in the test manual statistical evidence that two test forms are equivalent. Two types of data are usually reported—norms and correlations. When separate norms have been computed for each form, a glance at the relative positions of means or medians will tell you whether the group tested did better on one form than the other, and if so, how much better. Correlation of each student's performance on both forms will yield an *alternate form reliability coefficient.* Coefficients of .90 or greater are good evidence of equivalence.

If you are satisfied with evidence of equivalence of forms—and if you feel your audience will be as well—then you can compare pretest-posttest and time series scores as if students were being retested with the same instrument. Where evidence of equivalence is *weak,* build insurance against non-parallelism into your evaluation: The first time you administer the test, randomly divide program students or classrooms in two and give, say, Form A to one half and Form B to the other, keeping a record of which students took which form of the test. Then when it is time to post- or retest, give those who had taken Form A Form B, and vice-versa. In this way, you will prevent any small differences between the forms from affecting your comparison of results on different occasions or for different groups. Effects from an easier form will wash out in the *group* data.

Reporting time series scores from norm-referenced tests. Figures 12 and 13 describe graphs for reporting results of longitudinal and successive time series measures. Figure 12 shows the results from two subtests of a norm-referenced test—language arts and math computation—administered

Figure 12. Time series trend graph showing mean raw scores from six administrations of language arts and math computation subtests of the Comprehensive Abilities Test, Form J, to samples of program students

Figure 13. Median percentile ranks of successive seventh grades on language arts and math computation subtests of the Comprehensive Abilities Test administered over a six-year period

by a formative evaluator to samples of students six times over the course of a 7th grade language arts program. The program was initiated during the 14th week of school. You will notice that the raw scores of students on both subtests rise over the course of the school year. The slope of the language arts gain, however, begins to *steepen* after initiation of the program. This gives good evidence that the language arts program, and not changes in the general school environment or in the particular pool of students with whom the program was introduced, brought about the observed change in scores over time. Notice that the evaluator in this situation controlled for memory effects upon retesting by selecting *samples* of students at each testing occasion. This strategy works with as few as 30 or 40 students per site. Randomly pulling a few students to test rather than measuring everyone is also kind to your budget and to teacher morale.

The same graphing method works with a successive groups time series design. Figure 13 shows median percentile ranks[33] on language arts and math computation subtests at the end of a school year for successive

---

33. Sometimes the urge to report norm scores, when they are available, will overwhelm this chapter's admonition to graph only raw scores. Norm scores, after all, are easy to interpret. In these instances, consider this advice: norm scores more accurately reflect raw scores among students who are scoring in the middle range— around the 50th percentile, the 5th stanine, or with z-scores between -1 and $+1$, etc. Inaccuracy is less likely when you are dealing with average performance. But why chance it? Maybe the best thing to do is report the raw scores too, compare the graphs, and educate everyone concerned!

groups of students. The same norm-referenced achievement test in this case has been administered six years in a row.[34]

Reporting pretest-posttest results from norm-referenced tests. You can report scores on standardized tests using a table like Table 13. Scores displayed in the table represent a situation in which the *same test* has been given as both a pre- and posttest. The t-test tests the significance of the difference between mean pre- and posttest raw scores. It is a t-test for matched groups.

TABLE 13

Mean Pretest and Mean Posttest Reading and Math Scores
for Schools in the XYZ Program

Group	n[a]	Pretest	Posttest	t-test for difference between pre- and posttest
		Reading		
School A	401	59.4	64.3	3.8*
School B	720	50.2	70.5	12.2*
School C	364	40.9	60.2	4.5*
		Math		
School A	461	63.2	70.1	2.4*
School B	726	58.4	71.2	3.1*
School C	362	32.9	33.4	0.8

[a]Number present for both the pre- and posttests, and therefore the students on whose scores the t-test was calculated

*significant at .05 level

When interpreting these results, remind your audience of the following:

1. If the program lasted any length of time, a significant difference between a pre- and posttest would be nearly always expected anyway. Students do better on any particular test as they grow older and

34. Advice on examining, reporting, and discussing time series designs is contained in Fitz-Gibbon, C. T., & Morris, L. L. How to design a program evaluation (Chapter 5). In L. L. Morris (Ed.), *Program evaluation kit.* Beverly Hills: Sage Publications, 1978. See also Campbell, D. T., & Stanley, J. T. *Experimental and quasi-experimental designs for research.* Chicago: Rand McNally, 1966.

accumulate experience. However, you might find a situation such as that shown for Math, School C in Table 13: no significant difference between pre- and posttest scores. In this case, someone should look into what has been going on in this school. Was there a testing error, or are the students really making no progress?

2. A studied decision should be made about how seriously scores from the norm-referenced test should be taken. This decision should be based on:

- Awareness of how these tests are developed
- Assessment of the overlap in content of the test with the program being evaluated
- Description of the norm group with whom standard scores from the test are being compared

Reporting criterion-referenced test scores over time. If your measure is a criterion-referenced test, then you will be able to use the time series graphs described *only if you can represent the results of the test by a single number.* Converting criterion-referenced test results into single numbers would demand:

- Grouping objectives and then computing the mean number of students mastering each group
- Computing a raw score covering groups of objectives which are of about the same importance or deal with similar subject matter
- Using a single raw score from the entire battery if its objectives are of about equal importance

These are discussed under Question 4.

If you have gone to the trouble, however, of collecting information objective by objective, then you have much richer data about how the program students perform than can be communicated through a single number or graph. Your analysis should reflect this richness of information. Presenting criterion-referenced test results objective-by-objective is discussed in detail in the next section.

Question 4: To what extent have program objectives been attained?

Results from criterion-referenced tests are usually analyzed in terms of objectives. This analysis, however, can take several forms. Four ways to answer Question 4 are described in this section:

- Comparing results on each objective, either between groups receiving different programs or for the same group before and after instruction
- Comparing the number of objectives mastered per group

- Comparing amounts of time required by students to master objectives

- Reporting which objectives were mastered by many students and which were mastered by only a few *in a single group* and *at a single testing*

Chapter 2, pages 36 to 39, described a procedure for using a *norm-referenced test* to measure attainment of program objectives. As you can see from the procedure, objectives-based analysis of the results from most norm-referenced tests is extremely difficult. This is because of uncertainty about precisely which program objectives, if any, are measured by particular items and because the test may lack a sufficient number of items for drawing conclusions about most objectives. Criterion-referenced tests, if they are well constructed, should not present these problems since they are *designed* to be interpreted in terms of objectives.

Comparing results on each objective, either between different groups or at different times. In general, it is not appropriate to perform tests of statistical significance for differences in scores for a single objective. The comparisons you make, therefore, will have to be informal, relying on discussion of tables and graphs. *Bar graphs* are especially useful for presenting data about achievement of an objective. Each bar can represent the *percent of students passing* one objective if data have been reported per student or the *mean percent passing* if data have been aggregated by sites such as schools or classrooms. A glance at the graph reveals the program's strengths and weaknesses.

The example in Figure 14, page 135, shows results from the Compute-It and Think-Alot math programs for clusters of related objectives. Note that the passing rates for speed tests (Objectives Cluster A) were generally below 60% for both programs. It appears that the Compute-It program was more successful at teaching sets (Objectives Cluster B) and considerably more successful at teaching decimals (Objectives Cluster D). Looking at Cluster D, you might guess that the Think-Alot students did not receive instruction in the last five decimals objectives. Think-Alot appears to have produced better results, however, with fractions (Objectives Cluster C); perhaps more time was spent on that subject.

Results per objective could also be presented as *mean raw scores* on each objective for each group. If you wanted to see whether either program produced better *overall* results on the speed tests, for instance, you could average the raw score means for Objectives Cluster A.

When you discuss results portrayed as a mass of objective-by-objective comparisons, give foremost consideration to the *educational significance* of differences in performance. If the experimental group did better than the control group, how much better? If the differences are presented in

Figure 14. Posttest results from two math programs for four clusters of objectives

terms of percent of students passing, then what percent difference would make you sit up and take notice? If you are averaging raw scores per objective, then what does the difference mean in terms of proportion of items right, and how much of a rise in that proportion would satisfy you?

Differences between the *pretest and posttest* performances of a single group can be shown objective-by-objective in a similar way. Table 14 and Figure 15 illustrate common methods for displaying changes in a single group's mastery of objectives from pretest to posttest. The table shows the *mean percent of students in program classrooms* achieving 12 program objectives at pretest and posttest. Figure 15 graphically displays the same data. You can see from the figure that performance actually declined from pretest to posttest on objectives 1, 2, 9, 10, and 11, so the program is failing to teach some objectives. On the other hand, the number of students mastering objectives 5, 6, and 7 nearly doubled and rose to almost 70% for objective 5. If the program devoted much instructional time to these objectives, it may be sensible to credit the program with these improvements.

TABLE 14
Mean Percent of Students in Program X Classrooms
Achieving the Twelve Objectives
at Pretest and Posttest

Group	Objective #											
	1	2	3	4	5	6	7	8	9	10	11	12
Ninth grades (n=23)												
pretest	91	76	34	33	38	16	13	7	56	16	22	0
posttest	77	62	43	41	66	35	30	11	30	7	7	2

Figure 15. Mean percent of students in Program X classrooms achieving the twelve objectives at pretest and posttest

The quality of results from *a single group* can be more easily judged if they are compared against expected mastery levels set while the program was being planned. Where goals have been set regarding the percent of students who should pass various objectives, you can graph results by grouping objectives as in Figure 16. The graph shows that some objectives have a goal of 100 percent passing. In basic education, for instance, it might be decided that all students should be able to read pill taking instructions competently or know how to make change. For some objectives, and for a particular grade level, an 80 percent pass rate might be set as the goal, and other objectives might be expected to be attained by only 20 percent of the students. Such might be the case with "enrichment" skills. You can see from Figure 16 that the goal of 100 percent passing was not reached for objectives 2 and 11; the goal of 80 percent passing was not achieved for objective 6; all the 20 percent objectives for enrichment were achieved; and 3 goals had already been achieved at the time of the pretest—objectives 4, 5, and 22.

Figure 16. The achievement of program objectives showing different goals for the percent of students achieving the objectives

If you wish to call attention to the percent of students who moved from non-mastery to mastery on specific, highly critical program objectives, then you might consider including in your report a table such as Table 15. The table shows the pattern of student performance from pretest to posttest for important program objectives. The first row displays the percent of students mastering the objectives over the course of the program. This row reflects to some degree the effectiveness of instruction. The second row lists the percent of students for whom instruction on the objectives was unnecessary because they passed the pretest. Results in this column reflect little about the program except to show whether its objectives were appropriate for the student group in question. If too large a percentage of students appear in this row, then it could be argued that the program was a waste of time for a large proportion of the students. The third row shows the extent to which the program failed to come through for certain students—the ones who failed the posttest. Students are classified in this group whether or not they failed—or passed—the pretest. You might add a fourth row if you think that the program has done harm, leading to a decline in students' performance in the subject area; but this eventuality is usually unlikely.

TABLE 15
Percent of Students Showing
Three Different Patterns of Pre-Posttest Results
on Important Program Objectives

Pattern of Test Results	Objective					
	1	2	4a	5b	7	9
I Failed pretest/ Passed posttest	17					
II Passed pretest/ Passed posttest	45					
III Failed posttest	38					

Comparing the number of objectives mastered per group. For each student in a program or comparison group, you can obtain *a single score* that tells how many program objectives the student has mastered. These scores can then be aggregated to compute either the total or the mean number of objectives passed by students in different groups, or by students in the same group from pretest to posttest. Reporting a single score per group has several advantages:

- It is a convenient way to summarize results, particularly if you are assessing the achievement of many objectives.
- If you wish to *compare* the performance of different groups, or pretest and posttest results from the same group, the difference

between means can be tested for statistical significance in the same manner as more conventional total scores. See Table 12, page 126.

- Computing the mean number of objectives passed allows you to identify and characterize groups of students who fared particularly well or poorly on the posttest, and to produce gross measures of progress for groups which scored low, middle, and high on the pretest.

As you may have guessed, number-of-objectives-mastered scores also have disadvantages:

- They do not tell you *which* objectives were mastered and which were not.
- They treat all objectives as if they were of equal importance, though this frequently is not the case.
- Like all numbers based on mastery scores, they incorporate the arbitrariness that goes with setting cutoff points to define mastery.

Comparing amounts of time required by students to master objectives. Teaching toward mastery of objectives is based on the notion that any student can learn basic skills if given enough practice time. This naturally suggests a measure of how long it takes students to master critical program objectives. The *number of class hours* or *practice hours* it takes for, say, 50% of the students to attain *a particular set of objectives* could serve as a measure of program efficiency and therefore as a basis for program comparison.

Since the time measure must be based on mastery of *all* the objectives in a given set, the question of *which* objectives should comprise this set should be settled beforehand. These could be some of the program's most critical objectives, a randomly-chosen group of typical ones, a set representing particularly difficult-to-master skills, or perhaps a cluster of objectives that students failed on the pretest.

Time required to master objectives can also serve as an individual student score; it can be averaged and treated statistically like any such score. A time-to-mastery score is most suited to individualized learning programs and programs that use technological teaching aids such as language laboratories. In teaching situations where students do an indeterminate amount of out-of-class work, however, the amount of time spent on instruction or practice will be more difficult to determine. Also, unless tests of mastery can be mechanically or self-administered as soon as students are "ready," time measures will be limited by the fact that staff members are not continuously able to administer tests. If students have to wait to be tested, then time scores that a student obtains will become inaccurate.

Reporting which objectives were mastered by many students and which were mastered by only a few in a single group and at a single testing. Sometimes—particularly if your evaluation is formative—you will want to look at the results from a single test administration in order to locate objectives which students have failed to achieve. This information will give guidance to teachers and planners about which skills need attention. On the other hand, knowing which objectives *have* been attained by a large percent of the students is also useful to formative evaluators; it will prevent teachers from giving superfluous instruction, and students from doing unnecessary work. Both formative and summative evaluators may want to investigate *why* the program has or has not been successful in producing certain learnings. This may require taking a closer look at the program and its participants by investigating, for instance, student entry skills, student interests, teacher preparation, and the adequacy of program materials.

Analyzing student achievement of individual objectives requires first that you list program objectives and record beside each the number or percent of students who have mastered it, based on test scores. These data can be compiled or graphed in various ways. The simplest way is a table

TABLE 16
Mean Percent of Students in Program X
Achieving the Twelve Objectives at Pretest

Group	Objective #											
	1	2	3	4	5	6	7	8	9	10	11	12
Ninth grades (n=23)	91	76	34	33	38	16	13	7	56	16	22	0

Figure 17. Mean percent of students in Program X achieving the twelve objectives at pretest

which presents a single row of "percents passing" for each objective, such as Table 16. Figure 17 shows a bar graph illustrating these same results. Notice how much easier it is to survey the results from the graph than from the table.

You might also want to present results of this kind for each classroom, grade level, or other grouping of program participants. Table 17 shows data per objective in terms of percent of students passing in each *classroom*. Table 18 notes whether these percentages are greater or less than 80%, which was a goal the program sought to reach for each of the four objectives.

TABLE 17
Percentage of Students Passing the Objectives
in each of the Classrooms

Classroom	Writes name	Knows colors	Reads lower-case letters	Reads capitals
1	99	85	83	70
2	98	87	82	60
3	98	80	78	65
4	90	78	60	69
5	95	82	72	79
6	99	90	87	80
7	92	85	60	65
8	98	82	90	76
9	99	87	84	70
10	99	87	81	62

TABLE 18
Objectives Passed by 80% or More
of the Students in the 10 Classrooms

Classroom	Writes name	Knows colors	Reads lower-case letters	Reads capitals
1	+	+	+	o
2	+	+	+	o
3	+	+	o	o
4	+	o	o	o
5	+	+	o	o
6	+	+	+	+
7	+	+	o	o
8	+	+	+	o
9	+	+	+	o
10	+	+	+	o

KEY: + = objective passed by 80% or more of the students
       o = objective passed by less than 80% of the students

You can also *group* objectives based on the percent of students mastering them. Table 19 divides student passing rates into four levels and classifies objectives accordingly.

TABLE 19
Specific Objectives Mastered by
Varying Percentages of Program Students

Percent of students displaying mastery	Objective Numbers
76 - 100%	3, 11, 15, 16, 24, 25, 26, 33, 39, 42, 47
51 - 75%	4, 12, 14, 17, 18, 19, 22, 27, 30, 36, 43, 46
26 - 50%	1, 2, 6, 7, 20, 23, 28, 29, 34, 37, 38, 44, 45
0 - 25%	5, 8, 9, 10, 13, 21, 31, 32, 35, 40, 41

In much of this section, it has been assumed that cut-off scores per objective are used to make *pass/fail* judgments only. However, there is nothing sacred about a two-way distinction, and you could identify three or more levels of performance per objective. Table 20 shows three-way outcomes for seven objectives on a unit test administered to 135 students. Not shown in the table are the criteria used for deciding what constitutes low, middle, and high performance. These criteria, chosen by the staff or the evaluation's audience, would be expressed as numbers of items per objective.

A table like this is useful for formative evaluation. It allows decisions about satisfactory performance to be made based on how many students scored at each level. Objectives needing remedial attention can be located quickly. In this case, a standard was set such that fewer than 27 students (20%) showing low performance and 81 or more of the students (60% or more) performing high on the objective would be considered satisfactory by the staff. They would not attempt to revise instruction for that objective unless there were other strong reasons—say, from interview data—to do so. On the other hand, if either condition were violated—27 or more in the low column *or* 80 or fewer in the high column—then the staff would not be satisfied, and an attempt would be made to locate the program deficiency and correct it.

TABLE 20
Number of Students Showing
Different Levels of Test Performance
on Seven Objectives (n=135)

Objective	Level of Performance			Satisfied?
	Low	Middle	High	
#1	23	20	92	YES
#2	0	15	120	YES
#3	95	25	15	NO
#4	29	31	75	NO
#5	56	27	52	NO
#6	37	12	86	NO
#7	0	125	10	NO

Although the question of satisfaction in the table is always answered YES or NO, the staff might also have expressed different degrees of satisfaction or dissatisfaction. While performance on both the first and second objectives is satisfactory, for instance, performance on the second is very satisfactory indeed. Similarly, performance on Objective #3 is more than unsatisfactory; it is dismal. Variation in the proportion of students who have not achieved an objective may serve to focus greater staff attention on improving the program for some objectives than for others. It could also turn out that too many students in the low column will be more unacceptable than not enough students in the high column. Finally, primary attention may be given to revision for greater attainment on objectives that are considered by the staff to be prerequisite to success on subsequent objectives.

Question 5: How do achievement test results relate to student characteristics or program variations?

Answering this question means making statements of the following kind: "Students or programs with *this* pattern or degree of achievement tended to have *that* characteristic." Student characteristics that might be of interest include aptitude, socio-economic background, rate of attendance, and level of "entering skills"—skills in the subject matter in question which students possessed before entering the program. Relevant characteristics that vary within the program might be curriculum materials used, experience of teachers, class size, or amount of time allotted to particular kinds of instruction.

One way to examine how the program affected people differentially— depending on ability levels, gender, attendance rates, or whatever—is *to compare results from different subgroups.* Comparing the achievement of different groups might give you evidence that the program works well for certain kinds of students and not well for students in other categories. This is useful information for both summative and formative evaluation, and it can be displayed in the form of a table which presents headcounts or mean scores of various groups or categories. Table 21 shows one form that such a table might take.

TABLE 21
Format for a Table Classifying Students or Groups
According to Two Characteristics or "Factors"

		Factor 1			
		Level 1	Level 2	Level 3	Level 4
	Level 1				
Factor 2	Level 2				
	Level 3				

Factor 1 might be "textbook used" in a program in which teachers selected one of four alternative textbooks. The "level" in this case would simply refer to the choice of textbook. If there were no Factor 2, the table would consist of just one row of mean achievement scores for students in groups using different textbooks. If, say, linguistic background of students was of interest, however, the three categories of Factor 2 might be Oriental, European, and Other. The table would then display the variation in achievement among different language groups with different textbooks in this program. A factor, of course, may have any number of levels, and its division into levels should be based upon the presumed significance of each to the program.

You might use *level of performance* on an achievement test as one factor defining cells in Table 21. These levels could be low, middle, and high scores, for example, or scores above and below the median. First, establish the range of scores to be classified within each level. Then enter in the table the number of students whose scores fall within each level. *Low* might be a score less than 30, *Middle,* a score from 30-50, and *High,* a score above 50. In order to show a relationship, a second factor is required, such as the number of years that the student's family has lived in the district if this is of interest. The table will show whether the second factor appears to be related to how well students performed on the measure used. You can determine whether the relationship observed is likely to be due to chance by performing a test of statistical significance. Which statistical test is appropriate with such tables varies according to the kind of data they present. You should consult a basic statistics text to select the right statistical test.

When you want to measure the degree of relationship between two quantifiable factors such as scores, number of days in attendance, or number of objectives passed, you can also calculate a correlation coefficient. Table 9 in Chapter 5, page 110, shows the basic format for setting up data to begin calculating a correlation between two measures. The first column lists the *names of people*—students or other participants. The X column might record the person's achievement score, and the Y column, the number of years of formal schooling received by each person's mother. The correlation coefficient will then tell you to what extent students with better educated mothers performed better on the achievement test. Which among the many kinds of correlation coefficients you calculate will be determined by the type of numbers which measures X and Y have produced. You should consult a statistics text to locate the correct correlation coefficient.[35]

For Further Reading

On the topic of interpreting norm scores . . .

Angoff, W. H. Scales, norms, and equivalent scores. In R. L. Thorndike (Ed.), *Educational measurement.* Washington: American Council on Education, 1971, 509-600.

Gronlund, N. E. Interpreting test scores and norms. In *Measurement and evaluation in teaching.* New York: Macmillan, 1976, 387-424.

Lyman, H. B. *Test scores and what they mean.* Englewood Cliffs, NJ: Prentice-Hall, 1963.

---

35. See Fitz-Gibbon, C. T., & Morris, L. L. How to calculate statistics. In L. L. Morris (Ed.), *Program evaluation kit.* Beverly Hills: Sage Publications, 1978.

Appendix A
A Table for Program Test Comparison

Test_____   Subject area_____

Type: □ CRT □ NRT □ Unclear   Test level_____

                                        Grade level_____

1 Test item	2 Objectives that match item	3 Importance of objective					4 Item content and format analysis		
		1	2	3	4	5	0	1	2

Rated by_____

Date_____

| box A | Total # of program objectives used for selection |

5 Item appropriateness for students			6 Product of columns 3, 4, and 5	7
0	1	2		Summary figures

1 Test item	2 Objectives that match item	3 Importance of objective					4 Item content and format analysis		
		1	2	3	4	5	0	1	2

5			6	7
Item appropriateness for students			Product of columns 3, 4, and 5	
				Summary figures
0	1	2		

1 Test item	2 Objectives that match item	3 Importance of objective					4 Item content and format analysis		
		1	2	3	4	5	0	1	2

box B   Total # of items on the test

box C   # of *different* objectives listed

5 Item appropriateness for students			6 Product of columns 3, 4, and 5	7
0	1	2		Summary figures
				Grand Average Grand Tally (box D) ÷ total # of items on the test (box B) =
				Index of Coverage # of objectives listed in column 2 (box C) ÷ total # of program objectives (box A) =
				Index of Relevance # of products in column 6 (box E) ÷ total # of items on the test (box B) =

box D	Grand Tally

box E	# of products in column 6 > 0

A Reminder of Some Common Item Construction Errors*

You might ask these questions in order to suggest ways of improving your own tests—or for evaluating the quality of the items on tests that you have purchased.

Questions Concerning the Quality of Essay Items

- Could it be that the question requiring an essay response would be more easily answered and scored through another type of item?
- Would a large number of brief essays answer the question more easily than one or two extended essays?
- Is the question ambiguous? That is, does it fail to clearly and accurately explain the depth and extent of the answer that is desired? For instance, does it neglect to mention how many reasons, examples, arguments, etc., are expected in order for the answer to receive full credit? Does it explain what it means by "describe," "outline," "state," or "compare"? Does it neglect to accurately explain what type of answer will receive full credit?
- Is the question too broad to be covered adequately in the time allotted?

Questions Concerning Short Answer Items

- Is the statement to be completed too ambiguous to limit the correct answer to one or two specific words or phrases?
- Does the statement leave ambiguous the type of answer called for? The sentence "was found in—," could be answered, for instance, by either a date or a location.
- Do short answer statements leave blanks of differing lengths, or indicate the number of letters or words to be filled in by broken lines?
- Does the omitted part of each question come in the middle or at the beginning of statements rather than at the end where it belongs?
- Do items contain extraneous clues from grammatical structure, length of blank space, use of the article "a" or "an"?

---

*Many of the questions in this appendix were suggested by a document distributed by the New York State Education Department, Albany (1968) entitled *Improving the classroom test.*

- Could the type of information required be better handled through another type of question?
- Do items which require computation fail to describe the sort of answer required? For instance, do they neglect to explain the form in which fractions and decimals will be accepted, or whether units such as square yards or meters per second must be included in the answer?

Questions Concerning Multiple Choice Items

- Is a multiple choice format inappropriate to the type of information desired?
- Is the language of the item complex or unclear, perhaps containing unfamiliar vocabulary?
- Do items have more than one correct answer?
- Do items concern several central issues at once rather than a single one?
- Does the stem contain negative statements which have not been emphasized?
- Do responses or choices come at the beginning or the middle of the stem rather than at the end where they belong?
- Are response alternatives grammatically inconsistent with *the stem*?
- Are response alternatives inconsistent with *one another*?
- Are some response alternatives implausible or easily eliminated by students who lack the information tested by the item?**
- Are the response alternatives arranged in an illogical or confusing order?
- Are the response alternatives interdependent or logically overlapping?
- Do the response alternatives include extraneous clues due to grammatical inconsistencies or length of response? Are the correct answers, for instance, generally longer than the incorrect ones?
- Is the *none of these* option used inappropriately?
- Across items, is the correct answer among alternatives likely to be found in the same position much of the time? For instance, is the correct alternative nearly always in the middle position?

Questions Concerning True-False Items

- Are items indefinite or ambiguous in meaning?
- Is the true-false format inappropriate for obtaining this particular type of information?
- Are the items based on statements which have exceptions and qualifications which prevent them from being clearly true or false?
- Are the items based on opinion rather than fact?
- Is the central point of each question obscured by qualifications or difficult wording?

**Pay particular attention to this problem when looking at reading tests that present a short passage and then require students to answer a set of multiple choice questions about what they have read. Researchers have shown that many students can score better than chance on these items without reading the passage! A thorough discussion of this item characteristic can be found in Pyrczak, F. A note on measures of the passage-dependence of reading test items. *Reading Research Quarterly*, 1975-76, *11*(1), 112-117.

- Do the items contain statements that are partly true and partly false?
- Do items contain trick questions?
- Do items contain negative statements which are not properly highlighted?
- Do the items contain give-away determiners such as *always* and *never*?
- If examinees will be required to correct the error in a true-false item, does the item fail to indicate which portions should be corrected?

Questions Concerning Matching Items

- Do the premises and responses contain heterogeneous lists combining diverse types of responses, rather than homogeneous lists as they should?
- Are the lists of premises and responses too long?
- Are the matching lists arranged inconveniently? For instance, are responses long and complex rather than just a few words?
- Are directions ambiguous about the basis upon which lists are to be matched? Do the directions fail to mention, for instance, whether a single premise can be matched with more than one response?
- Do the matching lists contain extraneous clues due to, for instance, grammatical construction, or verbal associations?
- Is the list of responses the same length as the list of premises so that students can gain points through the process of elimination?

Index